The
Gerbil

An Owner's Guide To

A HAPPY HEALTHY PET

Howell Book House

IDG Books Worldwide, Inc.
An International Data Group Company
Foster City, CA • Chicago, IL • Indianapolis, IN • New York, NY

Howell Book House
IDG Books Worldwide, Inc.
An International Data Group Company
919 E. Hillsdale Boulevard
Suite 400
Foster City, CA 94404

For general information on IDG Books Worldwide's books in the U.S., please call our Consumer Customer Service department at 800-762-2974. For reseller information, including discounts and premium sales, please call our Reseller Customer Service department at 800-434-3422.

Library of Congress Cataloging-in-Publication Data
Siino, Betsy Sikora
The Gerbil/by Betsy Sikora Siino
    p.cm—(An owner's guide to a happy healthy pet)
    Includes bibliographical references
    ISBN: 1-58245-156-7

Library of Congress Catalog Card Number: 97-071179

Manufactured in the United States of America
10 9 8 7 6 5 4 3 2 1

Series Director: Susanna Thomas
Book Design by Michele Laseau
Cover Design by Iris Jeromnimon
External Features Illustration by Shelley Norris
Photography: All photography by Eric Ilasenko
Production Team: David Faust, Heather Gregory, and Heather Pope

Contents

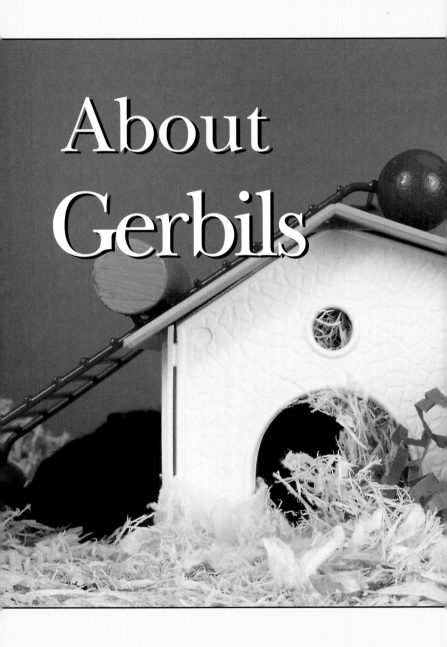

About
Gerbils

part one

External Features of the Gerbil

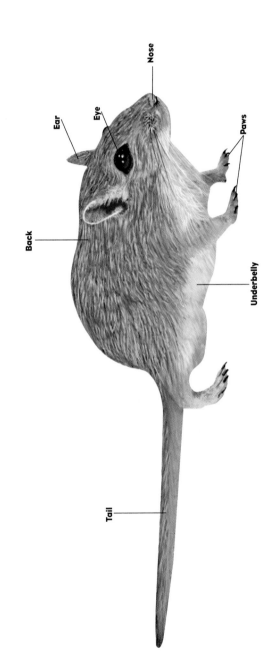

Nose

Eye

Ear

Paws

Back

Underbelly

Tail

chapter 1

What Is a Gerbil?

You're probably well aware a gerbil is one of those cute furry little animals that inhabit countless elementary school classrooms and children's bedrooms from coast to...well...almost coast, right? Simple. But it isn't that simple. Delve a bit deeper into the world of the gerbil, and you indeed find a cute furry little animal, but one who also happens to boast an endearing personality, a fascinating social structure, and a charter mem

bership in one of the animal kingdom's largest and most successful families. Once you know all there is to know about this wee critter, you may find that you're even more anxious to invite one, preferably two, to share your home.

Meet the Rodent Family

Before we get to know the gerbil, it's wise first to get to know the illustrious family to which he belongs: the rodent family. It's amazing to ponder the fact that approximately half the planet's mammals are rodents—a testament to both their rapid breeding rates and their resilience in the face of heavy eradication by most of the world's predators (particularly the human predator) since mammals first walked the earth. Given their numbers and their survival skills, were the world's rodents to join forces and decide to take over Mother Earth, they might just succeed. Scary thought, eh?

The word rodent comes from the Latin word *rodere,* which means "to gnaw." That is your first clue as to what is probably the most profound shared characteristic of this family—not to mention the characteristic with which those who have found their kitchens infiltrated by mice are intimately familiar. These critters are graced (or cursed, depending on your point of view) with amazing incisor teeth.

These teeth, the rodent's most valuable tools, continue to grow throughout the animal's life, permitting him to retrieve food wherever it may be, from the interior of a nut's hard shell, to the contents of a cardboard breakfast cereal box in the pantry. They also come in handy for basic construction work: for tearing into a wall of your home, for example, to gain access to a warm garage where you store your supply of dog food in a heavy plastic airtight container, which won't be airtight for long. By grinding against tooth surfaces on the lower jaw, the incisors remain sharp as razors and ready to tackle anything the rodent deems chewable, which would include most items and materials he encounters in his daily life.

The gerbil is a member of the resilient rodent family, with incisors that grow throughout his life.

The ever-growing incisors are a marvel, a true miracle of nature, and the key to a rodent's survival, but so must they be constantly maintained. The rodent just plain enjoys gnawing, even when it would seem to us that no culinary reward lies at the end of his efforts, as occurs when he gnaws with abandon on a stray block of wood or a cardboard tube placed in his cage. But beneath that enjoyment, he also knows inherently that he must gnaw to keep his teeth, his prized possessions, honed and healthy. Allowed to grow without benefit of maintenance gnawing, those incisors will just keep on growing, resulting in an animal who cannot eat and who suffers great pain from overgrown, possibly skin-piercing, choppers.

The reproductive capabilities of rodents have made them excellent survivors through the ages.

Also phenomenal are the rodents' performances in the breeding department. Most reach breeding age within weeks of their birth, and from then on, if proximity and housing permit, they will reproduce at incredible rates. Some will even raise two large litters only weeks apart in age at the same time. Wild rodent species have withstood drought, famine, habitat destruction, high-tech extermination efforts, temperature extremes—the whole gamut—and there's no doubt these animals' reproduction capabilities are what have kept them so prosperous and so populous, often exasperatingly so. Our species has attempted for centuries to drive many rodent species to extinction, but to no avail.

Despite the frustrations they can cause us—and the money we spend in our attempts to eradicate them—deep down we can't help but admire the profound adaptability of rats, mice, hamsters and such that comprise the rodent family. These are certainly not the most beloved animals on the planet. One might even venture to suggest that they, as a family, are the most reviled, primarily because many of them—unlike equally reviled snakes and other animals—live in such close proximity to humans. Many a rodent species learned ages ago that life could be easier when shared with humans, whether the humans wanted to share or not (and most humans would rather not). Though their brains are small, these are sharp creatures and world-class opportunists. They know what must be done to survive, and they're willing take any drastic steps necessary to ensure they do just that. And they always will. We might as well admit it: Where survival is concerned, rodents are the dominant clan.

Gerbil As Rodent

On the rodent spectrum, the gerbil in his natural wild state is a unique entity among his rodent brethren. The gerbil we speak of here is the Mongolian gerbil, the one species of the almost ninety known gerbil species that we humans have deemed to be an appropriate pet.

Mongolian gerbils were unknown to humans until their discovery in Eastern Mongolia by European explorers in 1867, so we have not known this critter long. Therefore, unlike many of his rodent cousins—the mouse and rat, for example, to whom the gerbil is closely related in his pet role—the gerbil's evolution has not developed in a long and arduous process alongside that of the human species. Nevertheless, get to know the gerbil, and you'll soon understand just why we chose to offer this humble, relatively unassuming rodent a formal invitation to join our households. You'll soon see him for the unique entity, the special member of both the rodent family and the pet family, that he is.

The Mongolian gerbil, named of course, for the region in which he was originally discovered, is a proud member of his own illustrious family within the larger family of rodents. This smaller group—also known as *jirds,* an Arabic word used to describe desert rodents—is comprised of those aforementioned ninety species that hail from various, usually arid, desert regions of Asia, the Middle East and Africa.

Most of these unique creatures, without human intervention or pressures, have evolved into some rather interesting animals. In a relatively short period of time, through a combination of experience with captive gerbils and limited research into wild gerbils, we have

Most pet gerbils today are descendants of Mongolian gerbils discovered in 1867.

gained a fairly clear view of who the Mongolian gerbil is. On the other hand, most of the other species of gerbils and jirds have remained somewhat elusive (the exception being those few, such as the Shaw's jird, who are beginning to find homes with experienced gerbil keepers).

It's a safe bet that even though some of these more unusual, and typically expensive, species have been "tried" as pets by gerbil keepers who know their Mongolian cousins, most gerbil and jird species would prefer to retain their elusive, free-roaming status.

A Unique Mongolian

As for our Mongolian friend, he is known to more scientifically minded folks as *Meriones unguiculatus,* to purists as the Clawed Jird, and to romantics fluent in Latin as "Little Clawed Warrior." Despite the latter title—which the species may have earned when someone witnessed the vicious battles that can ensue when a strange gerbil is introduced into another gerbil's established territory—the Mongolian gerbil is actually a quiet, gentle, friendly, relatively clean creature with kangaroo-like hind legs (for jumping away from and kicking sand in the faces of predators) and a long tail. Would-be rodent owners often do not favor long tails on their pets, but the gerbil's tail transcends that prejudice, for it is abundantly furred and even sports a soft tuft of hair at the end, reminiscent of a whimsical illustration that might have sprung from the mind of Dr. Seuss.

Evolving in a harsh, arid region of the world, the gerbil blossomed through the ages into a fascinating character, an identity enhanced by survival-borne traits that modern-day pet owners tend to find irresistible, even if they don't happen to understand the origins of those characteristics. For starters, desert life is hard on any animal, particularly one that stands only a few inches tall, weighs almost nothing and would seem a natural target for any would-be predator, be it avian or mammal. Yet the rigors of desert life also tend to sculpt indomitable creatures that are testaments to the theory of evolution.

The wild gerbil, for example, typically boasts a coat color described as agouti, a combination of earth tones, black and white (the white typically appearing on the chest and stomach area), often existing together on a single hair strand. The cumulative effect of these combined color bands provides the animal an effective coat of camouflage against the backdrop of his native territory. Having evolved in a very dry, often frigidly cold region, that coat covers a rather pleasingly plump, and thus naturally heat-conserving, physique, accented by relatively small ears with excellent hearing capabilities, an ever-twitching nose with a decent sense of smell, and large eyes. Also distinct is his somewhat thick muzzle that lends the gerbil an endearing expression and an overall appearance that sets him apart from the classical profile of the mouse, the rat, or even the hamster.

Indeed beyond his admirable technical adaptations, there is something decidedly unique about the Mongolian gerbil's appearance. Compared to the somewhat sleeker, more classically proportioned mouse or rat, the gerbil presents an image that can really only be described as adorable. Chalk it up to the somewhat largish head; the vivid, luminous eyes; the position and shape of the ears; certainly the soft brushed tuft at the end of his tail; perhaps the thickish shape of his muzzle. Whatever it is, the gerbil's sweet appearance, complementing an equally sweet temperament, tends to be one that is difficult for most of us to forget.

Upon your first meeting, your initial impression of the gerbil might be that of a timid, shy little animal, but remember that his first impression of you might genetically remind him of the large birds of prey and such who have targeted his gerbil ancestors for dinner since the dawn of ger-

One of the gerbil's favored attributes is his abundantly furred tail.

bil time. Your job as gerbil caretaker is to earn his trust and convince him you are not an owl who will be swooping down when he least expects it and carrying him off to some unknown and horrifying fate. Were he truly threatened by a predator, his best defense would be to run, preferably into his nearby burrow, and if all else failed, to kick sand into the face of his attacker with those powerful kangaroo-like legs. But powerful legs or not, you'll understand why he might be a bit cautious about staying out of trouble.

Mongolian gerbils, unlike their many nocturnal gerbil cousins, are diurnal, meaning that, like humans, they are awake by day and sleep at night. Residing in areas of such extreme temperatures in the wild, they tend to venture out of the subterranean colonies they call home to search for food at dawn and dusk. In captivity, however, where food is plentiful and they need not search for it on their own, gerbils are flexible in their daily scheduling habits. If you happen to work at night, your gerbils will, in most cases, be happy to adapt their schedules to yours to ensure togetherness, assuming of course, you have earned their trust and respect.

The gerbil's native diet is essentially vegetarian-based, though in arid, desert regions, one takes what one can find, and the wild gerbil may be inclined at times to supplement his preferred leafy, seedy vegetarian fare with an available insect or two. Though his evolution-

ary background does not involve intimate, opportunistic involvement with humans, as is true of mice and rats, in culinary habits, the gerbil shares the adaptability of all his rodent cousins—and, of course, the ever-growing incisor teeth and rapid reproduction rates.

The gerbil is a hardy little animal, whose system conserves water efficiently to the point of producing minuscule amounts of urine and sweat, and who may—no, make that *must*—be sustained on a simple diet, another offshoot of his humble desert roots. By remaining ever-cognizant of those humble roots, and re-creating them as

Think of how large we seem to our gerbil pets.

closely as possible within the human household, contemporary gerbil owners can make the most of their roles as caretakers of captive domestic gerbils.

The Gerbil's Wild Social Life

Though admired for the physical attributes that have made him a unique addition to the contemporary small-pet scene, perhaps the gerbil's most outstanding—and to some, most endearing—characteristic is his very social nature. This is a characteristic that is not common among all rodent pet species, or even all rodents, yet one that would-be gerbil owners must acknowledge immediately for both the physical and emotional well-being of their tiny pets. In other words, gerbils need other gerbils, so if you decide a gerbil is the pet for you, commit to getting at least two (more on how to make such an arrangement a success can be found in Chapter 2). Surviving amid a dangerous, arid environment, the Mongolian gerbil has blossomed into one of the most social, potentially friendly members of the rodent family—a trait that no doubt made him such a natural for life in human homes.

For gerbils, safety is in numbers, and that is precisely how the Mongolian gerbil lives in his wild homeland. Gerbils live in large, extended family groups in a network of well-planned, solidly constructed burrows beneath the ground. Within this domicile, you would find an area for sleeping, for raising newborns, for eating, for food storage, for eliminating and, no doubt, for play. Keep in mind, however, that our understanding of the life of gerbils in the wild is relatively limited. It's tough to study animals who lead complex lives underground, and, unlike their mouse and rat cousins, gerbils haven't made a career out of hitching rides uninvited on cruise ships or infiltrating restaurants and grocery stores in search of food. They have preferred a more natural, hidden rodent existence, always with an overriding allegiance to traditional family values that could put most politicians to shame.

The gerbil can be extremely social and friendly.

A given family group of wild gerbils typically consists of about twenty members who communicate through a distinct language of foot thumping, squeaking, wrestling and grooming behaviors. These traits are designed to retain order, to reinforce dominant and submissive roles, and to protect the colony. Without such behavioral protocols governing their societies, there would be chaos—and a convenient feast for neighboring snakes, owls and even rats.

Also fascinating is the makeup of the gerbil colony. This is a very progressive species as far as gender goes, and males are intimately involved in all the day-to-day workings within the colony—even in the raising of the young. Males, in fact, tend to be especially attentive to and protective of young or smaller gerbils, which owners often find quite enchanting. Colonies generally are comprised of several adult male gerbils, more adult females and a slew of youngsters of various litters. Each colony typically is dominated by a single breeding pair that researchers believe mate for life. Given the behavior of gerbils in captivity, it is also believed that females are the dominant gender and will not tolerate the attentions of competing females directed at their mates. And when we say "will not tolerate," we *mean* "will not tolerate."

GERBIL CHARACTERISTICS

The gerbil's domestic life mimics his wild ancestry. He:

- is highly social, preferring to live with other gerbils.

- conserves water efficiently, producing little urine or sweat.

- requires a simple diet.

Because of their speedy reproductive rates, and the fact that family members tend to remain in their home burrow even after they have matured, resulting in a large and affectionate extended rodent family, over time the family can grow too large for its family compound. At this time, younger members may leave the colony, presumably in search of new supplies of food, and end up starting new colonies of their own. They will usually do this only with members of their own clan, for though they are some of the rodent world's most sociable creatures, they are also somewhat xenophobic; they don't take kindly to strangers who wander into their territory and expect to become a new member of the clan. It won't happen, and some pretty ugly fights, even to the death, could ensue. If a marriage of gerbil lines is to occur, it must be between young gerbils—and the same, as we shall see, holds true within the territories of gerbil pets.

Gerbils As Pests

Xenophobia and jealousy aside, at this point we can't help but wonder just how an animal as sweet and harmless and seemingly ideal for life as a pet could ever be deemed illegal. Well, this has nothing to do with an aggressive temper or a predisposition toward viciousness, and everything to do with agriculture.

Some who make their livings growing and harvesting the nation's agricultural products—as is done to epic proportions in gerbil-unfriendly California, where gerbils are equal to contraband—fear that if gerbils are granted legal status, they might escape their homes and wreak utter, irreparable havoc on crops. Those who do not share such fears cannot help but reflect on the fact that rats and mice run wild among us, and hamsters are welcomed into California pet households with open palms, even though all share the same basic culinary habits as gerbils, and even though the hamster is a far more effective and willing escape artist than the gerbil. To date, herds of renegade hamsters haven't leveled valuable crops or established vast subterranean homes beneath the rich topsoil of the nation's agricultural fields, and it's doubtful that a few escaped gerbils would do that, either. Yet the fears remain.

chapter 2

Gerbils
As
Pets

Now that we have explored the character and biology of rodents and how they influence the personality of that little gerbil who will be residing in your home, we'll now move on and explore just how that tiny animal (or, preferably, that pair of tiny animals) will fit into a human household. The best way to make the relationship between you and a gerbil successful is to do all you can to understand the gerbil's world view. You will then not only be more realistic in your expectations, but also better prepared to make your resident gerbil a happy gerbil.

In the Beginning

Gerbils As Pets

It all began in the mid–19th century when European explorers ventured into the mysterious environs of Eastern Mongolia and discovered not only a vast and arid land, but also a tiny, sandy-colored animal living beneath the ground. This, of course, was the animal that would become the pet gerbil that we all know and love.

Recognizing immediately that they had found something special—it must have been those sparkling dark eyes or even the furry, tufted tail—these individuals set in motion the course of events that would lead to the gerbil's entrance into the contemporary pet world. Word spread, and over time, gerbils were taken into captivity. No doubt some hard lessons were learned along the way, not only about what gerbils need to survive, but also about their very complex social structures and their violent reactions to unfamiliar gerbils who infiltrate their territory. Even though today's pet gerbils have benefited from them, we'd probably rather not think about the gerbil casualties of those early experiments in gerbil keeping.

In time, interested parties gained the necessary knowledge and experience to raise gerbils, and by the 1930s, gerbils were being bred successfully in Japan, where they were kept primarily as laboratory animals. By 1954, gerbils had made their way to the United States, but not for very pleasant reasons. They had become laboratory animals here, too, imported precisely for that purpose, coveted, no doubt, for their sweet and tolerant temperaments.

It didn't take long, however, for news of that sweet and tolerant temperament to filter out beyond the

> ## WHAT IS A POCKET PET?
>
> When you hear the phrase "pocket pet," the image of a tiny animal peeking out from the pocket of a small child's jeans may pop into your mind, but that is an image that is indeed best left to the imagination. In the pet world, furry, warm-blooded animals of the smallest kind are typically referred to as "pocket pets," not because that is the preferred mode of housing for these critters, but because of their small size. Such animals include hamsters, rats, mice and, of course, gerbils, all of whom, despite their diminutive size, deserve clean, spacious, appropriate housing and tender loving care and handling.

laboratory walls to the ears of people who would rather live with animals as companions than do research experiments on them. By the 1960s, gerbils had become fully entrenched in the pet cultures of both the United States and Great Britain (except, of course, in those areas where agriculture departments deemed them *rodenta non grata*). Despite finding themselves in an environment that could not be more different from the arid atmosphere and underground burrows of their homeland, gerbils made themselves so at home in their newfound niche as pets, it seemed they had been a part of the pet landscape from the moment humans began keeping pets.

By the 1960s, gerbils transitioned from laboratory use to favorite "pocket pets."

How Gerbils Compare...

Though gerbils are naturally at home as pets and are pretty well-known both as many a child's first pocket pet and as the source of jokes that compare someone's attention span or intelligence to that of a gerbil, they have never been the most popular of the rodent pets. In fact, this sweet, quiet animal is often taken for granted, which is actually beneficial for a species whose charms are best reserved only for those who recognize and respect the species' special gifts.

Indeed, we would hope that forethought would go into one's choice of any pet, even one as small and easy to care for as a small rodent. No pet deserves to be viewed as inconsequential, even if it weighs only 2 ounces and makes barely a squeak. When one begins to consider taking a rodent for a pet, it's wise to acknowledge that all small rodents who live lives of domesticity are not created equal. Though most come into our homes with the same basic care requirements in terms of diet, toys and housing, each also boasts a distinct personality and world view. They deserve owners who understand that each rodent species is unique. For those would-be rodent owners who are new to this area of the pet world and are a bit confused by the possibilities, the following comparisons should help illuminate the differences between gerbils and their popular rodent pet cousins: rats, mice and hamsters.

...WITH RATS

Now for some people, particularly those who reside in New York City, the thought of taking a rat for a pet is repulsive. But those without such prejudices know that rats can be wonderful pets, and if you like rats, you'd probably like gerbils, as well. In fact, some believe the two look very much alike, though in truth the gerbil is typically much smaller than the rat—and, in all honesty, is not quite as intelligent as the rat (though few animals, even some human animals, are). And, of course, there is the issue of the tail. Many would-be rat owners are put off by the rat's long, somewhat scaly-looking tail. Such individuals might be soothed by the gerbil's alternative: a long, well-furred tail, which also happens to have an adorable puff of fur at the end.

The most dramatic similarity between rats and gerbils may be seen in the sociable personalities of the two, even though rats are less likely to escape or hide when allowed time at liberty from their cages. Most pet rats thrive best with ample human companionship, and though they are more gregarious and needy in this area than their gerbil cousins, gerbils, too, can learn to enjoy human companionship from those who take the time to earn their pets' trust. Many a gerbil and many a rat enjoy scampering up their owners' arms and finding a cozy perch on their shoulders, from which the resident rodent can enjoy an unobstructed view of the world.

But whether they are enjoying human companionship or not, gerbils must have companionship with others of their own kind—particularly others with whom they have grown up—so the decision to own one gerbil really means deciding to own a pair if you want what's best for your pet. This trait differentiates them from rats, as rats will reside with others of their own kind, but they are also perfectly happy living alone as long as their social needs are met by the people in their lives.

Rats and gerbils are both clean animals, yet gerbils tend to be more odor-free than rats. They are also quieter, less demanding, less prone to respiratory infections, and, as an unexpected bonus, gerbils may live longer than rats, too. While rats average a two-year life span, gerbils can make it to three and four, and possibly even five years old.

...WITH MICE

Gerbils also tend to outlive mice, who, like rats, tend to average a two-year life span—due perhaps to the fact that gerbils are typically less prone to the respiratory ailments that can quickly claim the lives of mice and rats. Gerbils and mice are both quiet and clean, and enjoy mutual grooming sessions, but because gerbils' bodies conserve more water and secrete less waste, they are more likely to earn the "odorless pet" title than are mice or rats.

Gerbils like to keep themselves and their surroundings neat and clean, and they tend to be more odor-free than rats and mice.

Gerbils rank higher than mice on the intellect spectrum, yet they share the intense social needs of their mouse cousins. Both gerbils and mice fare best when housed with others of their own kind—and both will overpopulate, and thus dangerously overcrowd, that very communal living situation in no time if you're not careful.

Where gerbils and mice diverge on the sociability scale is in the realm of human interactions. Often equated most accurately with goldfish, who would rather be seen than handled, mice would prefer to never be handled or touched by a human hand. Though at times handling and a change of scenery are necessary, particularly when it's time to clean the mouse house, mice are most content to remain safely ensconced within their cozy abode, cuddling with their mouse brethren.

Gerbils, on the other hand, don't at all mind some quality time spent with the people they know and love—assuming those individuals are well-versed in the protocols of gerbil interactions. In the absence of such manners, however, gerbils can be just as timid as their mouse cousins, and rather unforgiving of those who commit the crime of rough and noisy handling.

...WITH HAMSTERS

Though the gerbil was officially "discovered" approximately half a century before the hamster, the hamster has reigned for years as the more popular pet. It isn't that one is "better" than the other; the two are actually quite similar in size, ease of care and overall appearance, even though there are distinct differences between them. The hamster just seems to have a better public relations team—plus, she also doesn't happen to have a tail. For many would-be owners of rodent pocket pets, this latter attribute, or lack thereof, is the overriding factor that places the hamster immediately in the lead.

The stories of how gerbils and hamsters came to be pets in the first place are almost identical. Both were discovered in arid desert regions—gerbils in Eastern Mongolia, hamsters in Syria (gerbils discovered some 50 or 60 years before hamsters)—and the initial captive experience for both was as test subjects in research laboratories. Yet by the 1960s, both had been rediscovered, this time by pet owners seeking a quiet, easy-care pet that was appropriate for kids as well as adults.

Though gerbils and hamsters are often viewed by the general public as being interchangeable, these two small pets, though similar in some ways, are quite different in personality. As we have seen, gerbils thrive best when housed with other gerbils, yet the hamster prefers a solitary existence within her own enclosure— hers and hers alone. This is how each animal lives in the wild, and how each should be accommodated in the pet household. If you decide that you know better than Mother Nature and attempt to house a gerbil solo or hamsters in a crowd, you'll make what could be a fatal error in judgment for your pet—literally. So respect the differences, and respect each rodent pocket pet for who and what she is.

Gerbils in the Home

When compared to other rodents we humans tend to keep as pets, it would seem that, in some ways, the gerbil is the best-kept secret of the pocket pet world. We as a culture know of her existence, and we laugh at mis-

Who could make fun of this cutie?

conceived jokes about her empty head and hyperactive hopping abilities, but most of us don't know what it's really like to live with one of these animals. If more people did, it's a safe bet that most of the joking would come to an end.

It would be hard to deride a small animal so gentle, so quiet, so affectionate both to other gerbils and to her owners. The gerbil has apparently never learned the adage about the squeaky wheel getting the grease, so perhaps this naturally easy-going nature is what has led so many people to ignore the gerbil and to take her for granted. Yet those fortunate souls who have made this their chosen pocket pet know the truth. They have experienced firsthand the gerbil's abundant charms, and they can imagine no greater joy than hearing the soft thumping of a gerbil foot or the muted squeaks of a mutual gerbil grooming session gracing their home.

Indeed gerbils, best kept as same-sex, preferably related, pairs (more on this later), are delightful additions to the home. Watching the resident gerbils play and wrestle and groom each other— and playing with them out of their enclosure in a gerbil-proofed room of the house— can be as entertaining for the humans in the family as it is for the gerbils. What a privilege it is to be able to observe the interactions of these wee creatures in your very own house, to witness firsthand how creatures from a remote region of Mongolia probably behave in the wild. Make the most of the presence of gerbils in your home. First-time owners are often amazed at how such a tiny creature can enhance the inner glow of the home and of everyone who lives there.

Watching your gerbils at play in their enclosure can provide plenty of enjoyment for the entire family.

While gerbils bring a unique bit of nature into a household, they place few demands on the human members of their family. The gerbil is an easy-care pet with a pleasant and, as we have seen, very sociable personality. Keep her bedding fresh and her home clear of urine buildup, yesterday's dinner and caches stashed with old food, and she can be a relatively odorless pet, as well. All in all, the gerbil can be the perfect roommate—assuming that you also play the role of perfect roommate and ensure that she has a live-in gerbil roommate, as well.

Gerbil Character

Though gerbils are not far removed from a wild existence that was discovered a relatively short time ago—unlike, say, the dog, who was domesticated thousands of years ago—gerbils seem to have come to Earth with qualities custom-made for their ultimate role as family pet.

The gerbil's gentle nature has forged her reputation among those with a penchant for pocket pets as one of the sweetest natured of the rodent pets—and, frankly, of any pet. So gentle is this small animal, she is typically the least apt of any small rodent pet to bite the hand that feeds her—or plays with her, or cleans her domicile, or picks her up. She may nibble upon a trusted hand occasionally, but that's a gesture born of affection and curiosity, not the anger and fear that invokes a more violent response. A frightened or angered gerbil will indeed use those sharp gerbil teeth to bite, and then kick sand in your face to drive the point home.

Remain gentle and quiet in a very gerbil-like way yourself, however, and you will be the person the gerbil wants you to be, the person she wants to trust and spend time with. Though she will bond deeply with her cagemate—who is ideally one of her siblings of the same gender (a partnership designed both to prevent a gerbil population explosion and to maintain peace within the gerbil house)—she is always willing to share her attentions with a deserving human friend, as well.

Gerbils are also fastidiously clean animals. They demand that their homes remain clean and pristine—they prefer to have the premises divided into various "rooms," the eating area in one section, the bathroom in another, nest area in another, etc. They demand cleanliness of themselves, too. Gerbil roommates

---

BENEFITS OF GERBIL OWNERSHIP

Gerbils have distinct advantages over other rodent pets. These include:

- a relatively long life span.
- an assiduous habit of cleanliness.
- less demanding attention requirements.
- a higher resistance to respiratory ailments.

spend a great deal of time grooming each other, sometimes interspersed with bouts of playful wrestling. This activity keeps the gerbils happy and content, and it also reinforces who is the submissive member of the pair, and who is the dominant.

Making Your Gerbils Happy

Though gerbils are not as demanding as, for example, dogs are in the pet-care department (no daily walks required), there are certain needs you must meet to keep your small pets content and healthy. Simply look to the natural, wild lifestyle from which they hail, and you will have all the clues you need to become a successful gerbil keeper.

As we have seen, this social critter will want a buddy of her own species. Considering her genetic predisposition to xenophobia, finding a companion for her must be done carefully. These are also burrowing animals in their native state. Hint, hint: Supply her with an ample layer of healthy bedding in her home so she might partake joyously in the natural burrowing activities that are the right of every gerbil. Make sure, too, that the enclosure is large enough to house the resident gerbil—a 10- to 20-gallon glass tank for two gerbils, for example—to prevent potentially violent arguments and the onset of cabin fever. And, of course, make sure the enclosure is well-maintained to meet the gerbil's high standards of cleanliness.

A 10- to 20-gallon glass tank provides ample space for one or two gerbils.

Remembering again your pet's wild roots, keep her diet simple. Rich foods will only lead to an overweight, uncomfortable and possibly ill gerbil. Offer her fresh food every day, and remove uneaten food promptly to avoid spoilage and odor. Where water is concerned, you might actually wish to forget about those arid, desert

25

origins where water was scarce. Though wild gerbils may not require a great deal of water to survive, make sure your pet gerbils have a fresh supply available at all times.

In addition to behaving properly around your gerbils and handling them gently, supply these fun-loving critters with safe and appropriate toys (an exercise wheel designed for animals with tails and a hamster ball for out-of-enclosure exploring, for example). Allow them time out of their enclosure from time to time, too, but only if they are willing, and only in a room that is properly gerbil-proofed. This latter element includes keeping the family dog or cat out of the room, and generally keeping them away from the gerbils' tank or cage, as well. Needless to say, a small rodent that has evolved to protect herself constantly from birds and mammals intending to eat her is not likely to be comforted by the stares and salivation of a dog or cat whom the gerbil views, probably quite accurately, as a predator. The fright from such an encounter can actually cause the gerbil to experience a seizure or stroke, and you certainly don't want that to happen.

And, finally, your role as gerbil caretaker also mandates that you keep an eye on her health. Look for changes in condition or behavior that could indicate illness. Naturally, we will be going into greater detail about all these gerbil-keeping basics in the following chapters, but now you have a general idea of what you must do to keep your gerbils happy—and, in turn, healthy, as well. And remember, the undemanding, unassuming creature that is the gerbil isn't one to complain in the face of neglect. But she is prone to great stress, and stress in small animals can lead to serious illness. So stay dedicated to the job at hand, and let your conscience be your guide.

Gerbils and Kids

No discussion of gerbils as pets would be complete without mention of the relationship between children and gerbils. When many hear the word "gerbil," they automatically think of these animals as being ideal pets

for children. Indeed, children can be wonderful gerbil caretakers, but they also can be disasters at the job. Just ask all the gerbils who have been "sentenced" to the care of young children through the years and met premature ends, simply because so many people just naturally consider the gerbil to be a child's pet.

No offense to children, but most are not capable of taking on the full responsibility of a pet's care. Though the gerbil is relatively undemanding in her needs, we have seen how committed one must be to care for a gerbil properly, and it would be unfair to assign every one of those responsibilities to a child, especially a young child.

As with all animals, gerbil care by children should supervised by adults.

Unfortunately, this is what occurs every day in classrooms where, once again, gerbils are considered an ideal children's pet, this time in an educational environment. Because of her naturally sweet temperament, the gerbil is frequently taken into the classroom as the perfect vehicle for teaching kids about pet care. In some cases, this may be true, especially when classroom gerbils are kept in pairs and when their care is not assigned to a different child every week, which undermines the necessary consistency, but is assumed by the teacher, an adult who understands what this small animal requires. Children can learn about animal care just as effectively when an adult is caring for the animal.

About Gerbils

What is best for the classroom gerbil is also best for the gerbil who resides in a home with children. The adult must be the primary caretaker. Feel free to enlist the kids' help in feeding, watering, playing and cleaning the enclosure, and by all means teach the children how to handle the small animal gently and correctly. This way you not only ensure that the gerbils are receiving their proper and complete care, but also that the kids are learning how to offer that care, lessons they will retain for the day when they do find themselves the sole caretakers of pets of their own.

Such early lessons in pet care and handling can prove invaluable in molding a youngster's perceptions of animals and their well-being—and their regard for and treatment of animals in the future. Just make sure that the animal's care is carried out under adult supervision and responsibility. The result can last a lifetime. Just think of the stories you have heard through the years, fond memories shared by those who grew up with gerbils, those who have experienced firsthand the charms and magic of this sweet-natured animal. Though one of the pet world's smallest members, the gerbil's influence can be far-reaching indeed.

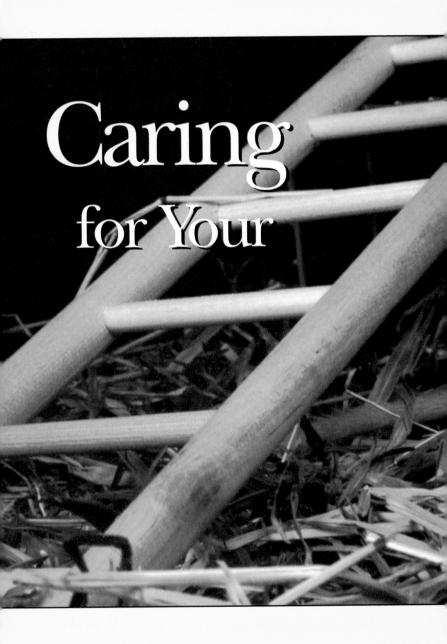

Caring
for Your

part two

Gerbils

chapter 3

Choosing and Preparing

for Your

Pet Gerbils

You will notice that the title of this chapter mentions gerbils in the plural rather than the singular. By this time, it should have become abundantly clear that gerbils are best housed with other gerbils and will probably live longer and healthier in such a situation. For the non-breeder and certainly for the beginner, the optimum multi-gerbil "clan" consists of a single-gender pair, who, ideally, have grown up together—a formula designed for both the well-being of the gerbils and the sanity of the household. So, in discussing that fateful process of preparing for and choosing a gerbil to join your family, we will assume that it is a pair you will be seeking.

On Becoming a Responsible Gerbil Owner

Purchasing a pet on impulse is never a good idea, but when the would-be pet is a small rodent, the prospective owners tend to be even more impulsive and less prepared than they might be for, say, a dog or a cat. The sad results are countless small animals whose fates include neglect, abandonment and unnecessary suffering. This would all be so easily remedied if potential pocket pet owners would take a moment at the first twinges of impulse and give the matter some thought.

Every pet, even a rodent pet, deserves a lifetime commitment. Now, with a gerbil you're not talking about a commitment that will last for the next decade or more, but it is a commitment just the same—and, unfortunately, one for which every interested party may not be prepared. Sure, the critters are adorable with those

The black gerbil is just one of over fifty color varieties available.

large round eyes, that tufted tail and that oh-so-sweet-and-friendly disposition, but caring properly for a pet involves more than simply admiring it.

Your first step, then, when you feel that first twinge of impulse coming on, is to take some time to evaluate honestly whether now is the right time for you to take on a pet and whether your lifestyle is currently up to the challenge. First, think about your work and travel schedules. The gerbil can be an excellent choice of pet for busy people, unless, of course, those individuals are so busy that they are gone for weeks or even months at a time. Think, too, about the configuration of your family. If you have young kids, great, but remember that their interactions with the gerbils must be supervised, and the animals' care must be a designated adult responsibility. Make sure that older kids, too, have been well-trained in the protocols of humane and gentle pet handling.

Caring for
Your Gerbils

Just ask yourself the pertinent questions. For example, are you willing to keep two gerbils instead of one? Do you have the time and inclination to feed the gerbils and remove uneaten food each day? Can you make the effort to keep the gerbil house and all its accessories clean and well-maintained? Are you willing to take your pets out for playtime? Are you willing to practice good manners with your pets, and treat them each day in such a way that earns their trust and respect? If your gerbil seems ill, would you be willing to consult a veterinarian with expertise in the care of pocket pets? And finally, why do you want a pet in general, and gerbils in particular?

The honest answers to these questions can tell you whether the gerbil is right for you, or whether maybe you should wait a while before inviting this, or any animal, to join your household. If you determine that, yes, the gerbil is the animal, the time is right and the family is ready for the commitment, then get ready, get prepared, and get started in your search for your new gerbil companions.

Preparing for the New Additions

Believe it or not, people purchase pets every day without knowing the first thing about their care. As we have seen, every pet, even every rodent pet, comes into the home with a distinct personality and care requirements, usually rooted in the type of lifestyle the species leads in the wild, and the type of region from which it hails. The first great favor you can do your gerbil pets is to get acquainted with what is unique about these animals, and what they require to thrive in a captive environment. Ideally, this should be done before any gerbils join your household.

The same holds true for gathering the supplies your new gerbils will require. Housing items, bedding, food, toys: These should all be assembled ahead of time, the animals' accommodations set up and made ready to receive the new gerbil inhabitants as soon as they cross the threshold of their new home.

Preparing both educationally and practically will help ensure that those first few days with new gerbils in the house will be as stress-free as possible for everyone involved. The animals can settle right into their new digs and start making themselves at home immediately, and you don't have to scramble around in a panic getting everything ready while simultaneously worrying about where the gerbils are, what they're doing, and whether you're remembering everything the books and pet-store clerks told you a gerbil must have to survive. Think ahead for everyone's benefit. Life will be much more peaceful for your forethought.

It's important to gather supplies for your gerbils before they arrive in your home.

Where to Find Your New Pet

Though it might be a most romantic start to your choosing a gerbil for a pet, you need not book passage to Mongolia to find a pair of these wee animals of your very own (and that, in fact, wouldn't be a good idea even if you could; captive-bred pets are always superior, and more humane, choices). There are plenty of, even too many, gerbils just waiting for new homes each day all across the country. The following are some of the more common sources of gerbil pets—although given this species' breeding habits, you may at this moment have gerbil-owning friends who have unexpectedly found themselves with available gerbil pups. Ask around—and perhaps share what you know about preventing such unexpected turns of events in the future.

PET SHOP

Probably the most convenient source of gerbil pets is the pet store. Even pet supply superstores that do not sell puppies and kittens often sell pocket pets of the rodent variety, and you may be able to find the pair you're looking for there. Unfortunately, not all pet shops are created equal, so deal only with a shop that is clean and sanitary, that carries what seem to be healthy animals, that boasts a knowledgeable staff (a definite plus when you're trying to figure out whether the gerbils are males or females) and that does not offer gerbils for sale who are younger than 6 weeks of age (gerbils should be allowed to remain in the care of their mother until that 6-week milestone).

WHERE TO BUY YOUR GERBIL

Whether you decide to acquire your gerbils from a pet store, breeder, animal shelter, a fair or show, it's important that you deal with people who demonstrate knowledge about your animals. They should be able to help sex your gerbils and provide specific advice about their care.

BREEDER

Given the natural ease with which gerbils breed on their own, it may strike some as humorous to think of someone purposely going out and breeding these animals. But gerbil breeders there are, and many of them are extremely dedicated to the well-being of Mongolian gerbils. Link up with one of these individuals—perhaps at a gerbil show held in conjunction with a county fair or someone you locate through the Internet—and you may discover that the breeder can be an excellent source of healthy, well-socialized, and perhaps uniquely colored gerbils. (Do remember, though, that just because someone presents a snazzy Web site on the Internet does not mean he or she is reputable, ethical or even knowledgeable when it comes to gerbils, so remain on your guard, ask for references, and let common sense prevail.)

The sign of a good breeder is someone who is obviously knowledgeable and contagiously enthusiastic about the care, health and socialization of gerbils, and who has plenty to say about about the uniqueness of each one of his or her own animals. Another positive sign is a breeder who is willing to mentor you through your first experience as a gerbil owner, who counsels you on the need to house these critters together, and who offers a money-back guarantee on his or her animals should the arrangement not work out for some reason. If you are fortunate enough to find such a breeder, but discover that he or she lives hundreds or even thousands of miles away, don't despair; most breeders will ship their animals humanely to new owners they deem worthy caretakers of their gerbil pups.

ANIMAL SHELTER

The animal shelter, like the breeder, might seem a puzzling source for gerbil pets, and, indeed, its inclusion here is not to suggest that every shelter will have gerbils available. But more and more shelters are offering small and exotic animals these days, animals that, just like their larger canine and feline counterparts, are left homeless by abandonment, neglect or similar tragedies. Should you decide you're ready to make some gerbils new members of your family, it doesn't hurt to call the local shelters in your area and see if they have any likely prospects available. You may be surprised—and amply rewarded.

FAIRS AND SHOWS

If you have ever been to a county fair, you may have happened to come across one of those unique events that is the gerbil show. Often held in conjunction with shows featuring other rodent pets, these are not only fascinating events, but also an ideal opportunity to meet rodent breeders—in this case gerbil breeders—and even a great many available gerbils all at the same time. These events also offer you the ideal opportunity to talk to the experts about gerbil care and to ask any questions you might have. Most of the people deeply involved with small animals as a hobby tend to be good, down-to-earth folks, ever eager to welcome newcomers and to share the wealth of their knowledge.

Of course, the gerbil show, if there is one scheduled, will not occur each day of the fair, so call ahead of time for the schedule of events and make sure you don't miss your window of opportunity. In some communities you might also find local magazines or newspapers that offer listings of animal-related events in the area. Check these listings for information about upcoming rodent and pet shows in your area, and make plans to get to know some gerbils and the people who love them. You may end up coming home with a pair of your very own.

WORD OF MOUTH

Even if your local animal shelter doesn't have any gerbils available, the staff may know of breeders in the area or other sources of gerbil pets. Some shelters actually act as an information center for people looking for all kinds of pets, even though the shelter itself does not officially house and offer animals other than cats and dogs.

The same can be true of veterinarians, especially veterinarians who specialize in the care of pocket pets. Such practitioners will typically know of any breeders in the area and can point you in the direction of individuals who are probably responsible in their endeavors, given the fact they consult a veterinarian for the well-being of their stock. You might also contact local pet-sitting services to see if they have any information on people with available gerbils. Owners of small animals often call pet sitters to care for their pets while they are away, these easy-care critters being ideal candidates for pet-sitting services. So once you decide gerbils are for you, start your networking. And good luck.

Choosing a Healthy Gerbil... or Two

Regardless of where you find your gerbils, the criteria for evaluating potential new pets are standard. These involve looking at the animals with a clear eye, beyond the cuteness or pity factor (the latter factor invariably springing from such thoughts as, "If I don't take them, they'll become snake food!"). Allow a cool head to prevail and look for the gerbils with the best potential for healthy and vital lives. The following guidelines should help.

THE FACILITY

Before you even look at the gerbils who may be going home with you, look around at the premises where they are being housed. The facility should be clean, as should the gerbils' individual enclosures (fresh bedding, clean food and water, no spoiled food, no unusual odor), and the gerbils should not be overcrowded in their habitats. Avoid gerbils from a filthy establishment, whether that happens to be a pet shop, breeder's home or animal shelter. Unsanitary conditions can cause illness and uncharacteristically aggressive behavior in gerbils, and those are not attributes you are probably looking for in your new pets.

AGE

Given their naturally social natures, gerbil pups should remain with their mothers until they are at least 6 weeks of age. This helps to prevent neurotic or atypical behavior that can occur when gerbils are taken away from their moms before they are ready. At that point, gerbils are considered emotionally and physically ready to leave their families (assuming they are not gerbils who will be remaining with the family throughout their lives) and find a comfortable new niche with a human family.

Being patient and knowledgeable when selecting healthy gerbils from reputable sources will help you avoid problems down the road.

You need not, however, take only a young gerbil as a pet. An older gerbil can adjust well to your home quite easily, too, especially if he is coming into your home with his longtime companion by his side. Success with any gerbil, young or old, relies on a dedicated owner.

As we know, this means someone who practices proper gerbil behavior when meeting a new gerbil and helps him to rehabilitate from any negative experiences he may have had in the hands of someone not quite as educated, patient and dedicated as his new owner.

GENDER

Gerbils are a female-dominated species, yet, being generally sweet-natured regardless of sex, both males and females can make excellent pets. The real issue is that of housing them in pairs, which is the superior setup for the well-being of gerbils in most households. Unless your goal is to launch a gerbil population explosion in your home (as has happened to many an unsuspecting owner who was either the victim of misinformation regarding a gerbil pair's genders, or who simply didn't think about the consequences of housing a male and female gerbil together), you would be wise to take the tried-and-true "single-gender-pair" advice seriously. (You will find more on identifying your gerbil's sex in Chapter 8, "Understanding Your Gerbils.")

TEMPERAMENT

As with gender, temperament, too, has much to do with a gerbil's social needs. A gerbil taken away from mom too early and housed solo is far more likely to be one of those rare specimens with a predisposition to biting. That is true, as well, for a gerbil who has been mistreated, subjected to rough handling and loud noises, or perhaps lifted by his tail from time to time.

Most gerbils are born with a friendly disposition, asking for nothing but respect and gentle handling to maintain that friendly demeanor. Some gregarious gerbils will literally beg for attention, jumping up on their hind legs and leaning up against the side of their cage or enclosure, although such outwardly affectionate, attention-getting invitations are more likely to occur after you have become housemates and gotten to know and trust each other. If, however, the gerbil behaves this way upon your first meeting, this may just be a case of love at first sight.

When evaluating the temperament of potential gerbil pets, first try to observe how they interact with each other. If they contentedly groom each other and share bouts of friendly wrestling, those are positive signs. If, on the other hand, you notice no affection between them—or even more dramatic signs like fighting, blood and such—this could simply mean that they were strangers thrown together in a cage rather than indicate an inherent temperament problem that will make them inappropriate pets. These gerbils may make lovely pets when separated and either reintroduced to each other or to another potential roommate according to the methods described in Chapter 8, "Understanding Your Gerbils." The aggressive behavior, whether ripe for rehabilitation or not, could also be a sign that these gerbils are in the care of people who either don't understand gerbils or simply don't care about the well-being of the animals in their care, so tread carefully.

Mutual grooming and play fighting can be positive traits in gerbils.

When you introduce yourself personally to the gerbils, you will have to give them the benefit of the doubt, especially if they have just awakened from a nap. Though friendly by nature, it usually takes even the most well-adjusted gerbils some time to get acquainted with and accustomed to the scents and touch of a new owner. For a personal evaluation, try placing your hand in their cage or enclosure, perhaps with a small treat (Cheerio or sunflower seed) in your palm, and keep it very still. Observe the gerbils' reaction. If they appear curious and venture forward to sniff, and perhaps even nibble, your hand, great. At this point, you may even feel confident attempting to pick up one of the wee creatures. If he is amenable, carefully lift him up, one hand supporting his underside and the other hand covering his back for security (he will let you know early on if this is unacceptable). Keep the interaction short, and, if possible, hold him above the bedding of his enclosure for safety's sake.

If the gerbils don't come forward to explore your hand, yet you notice a definite curiosity in the twitch of the nose attempting to catch your scent and a bright expression in the eyes, that is probably a good sign, too. The physical contact can come later, developed gradually as you earn the animals' trust and respect.

At this point, it's basic curiosity you're looking for. If, however, the gerbils appear depressed and listless, or their curiosity manifests as an aggressive lunge with teeth bared as if to attack, accompanied by foot thumping or an attempt to kick bedding material in your face, perhaps these aren't the gerbils for you. Such behavior, whatever its sad cause, is not what motivates most of us to live with these legendarily sweet-tempered animals. Rest assured a more even-tempered gerbil awaits your attention elsewhere.

OVERALL HEALTH

And now we come to that all-important responsibility of evaluating the overall health of potential gerbil pets—obviously a very critical department. While you probably won't be bringing a veterinarian who specializes in gerbil medicine along with you when it's time to choose your new pets, there are some pretty vivid signs that the layperson can look for that indicate whether or not a particular gerbil is as healthy as he should be.

First, look at the eyes: the windows to health as well as to the soul. They should be clear and bright, free of discharge. Healthy ears, too, should be free of discharge that can indicate the existence of parasites or infection. Beware of a runny or bloody nose, which could be the sign of a respiratory infection, and

drooling from the mouth. This latter sign could indicate an unbalanced bite, or, worse, a malformed jaw
structure, which can result in improper honing of the
ever-growing incisors, a life-and-death issue if the condition is severe. A gerbil afflicted with a malformed jaw
should be humanely euthanized; otherwise he will
have to have his teeth trimmed
periodically by the veterinarian to
prevent the pain and suffering—
and malnutrition—that can result
when a gerbil is physically inca-
pable of eating properly.

In addition to his proper jaw structure, the gerbil's coat should be
soft, smooth and uniform in tex-
ture, free of sores, lesions, tumors
or parasites. A matted, dirty or otherwise unkempt coat is the sign of a
gerbil who is not keeping up with
his grooming responsibilities, a
negative sign possibly indicating
poor health in so fastidiously clean
an animal. While small rodents
tend to breathe rather quickly, the
gerbil should breath smoothly and quietly, his breaths
uniform and clear. His typically well-rounded physique
should appear robust, stocky and muscular, and he
should move easily and painlessly through the bedding
of his enclosure.

> **IMPORTANT FACTORS
> IN GERBIL HEALTH**
>
> When selecting a gerbil, check for:
>
> - clear eyes.
>
> - ears free from parasites and
>   discharge.
>
> - nose and mouth free from
>   blood or drool.
>
> - properly formed jaw and
>   incisors.
>
> - soft, parasite- and lesion-free
>   coat.
>
> - uniform, quiet breathing.
>
> - healthy appetite and robust
>   form.

If you're lucky enough to observe the gerbil at meal-
time, regard a healthy appetite as a good sign, as well
as an enthusiastic interest in toys, mutual grooming
and wrestling. By the same token, regard signs of diarrhea, either in the enclosure or on the gerbil's rear
end, as a dangerous sign, one that should send you
looking elsewhere for your new pet. In fact, one sick
gerbil could mean that the rest of the gerbils on the
premises are ill, too. Therefore, part of your standard
evaluation should include observing all the gerbils in
the facility, not just those that catch your eye. You certainly don't want to bring your new pet home and find

that your first pet gerbil experience involves caring for
(and possibly losing) a very sick gerbil (or two).

A Gerbil of a Different Color

Considering the many factors you should evaluate
when looking for a pair of gerbils to take into your
home as pets, it would seem that color would be inconsequential. Technically, it is, for the roles that health
and temperament play in an animal's identity as a well-
adjusted pocket pet far outweigh coat color, eye color,
a particular spot on the head or tail, or similar external
appearances. Those involved in the so-called gerbil
hobby, however, have made color and the many variations that have been developed through the years an
interesting facet of the world of the gerbil, and one
that might attract the attentions of would-be owners.

From that original classic sandy-colored agouti coat that
blended like military camouflage with the arid, earthy
Mongolian backdrop of the gerbil's homeland, a vast
and ever-growing rainbow of colors and patterns have
been developed in contemporary captive gerbils, just as
they have in other rodent pet species. Most of these gerbil colors and patterns are genetic variations on the
original agouti coat with its white underside, and some
are variations on the black-coated gerbils, a color that is
relatively new to the gerbil color spectrum. Breeding
for colors and patterns is a fairly recent development in
the gerbil world, so the variety has not yet reached that
enjoyed by enthusiasts of other rodent species, such as
hamsters and guinea pigs. But breeders are working
feverishly to catch up, gathering as much information
as possible about the inner workings of genes and muta-
tions along the way. They are hoping eventually to
develop not only more colors and patterns, but also
new coat types and textures along the lines of those
found in hamsters and guinea pigs, such as satin, rex
and teddy bear (long-haired) varieties.

Gerbil Colors You May Find

What follows are some of the more common gerbil
colors and patterns you might run across in your

search, though with approximately fifty colors on the palate, this is by no means a complete list. Owners and would-be owners often find themselves captivated by a particular color, yet keep in mind that not every color and pattern, especially the newest additions to the gerbil color spectrum, is available in every area. For some, you may just have to wait. But remember: No matter what, health and temperament come first.

*The young
agouti gerbil.*

AGOUTI

This is the classic gerbil, the one originally discovered in the arid lands of Eastern Mongolia. He is a sandy-colored, black-eyed gerbil with a white or cream-colored tummy, and his sandy appearance is created by a sea of hairs, each one banded with a combination of black, yellow and brown.

ARGENTE GOLDEN/ARGENTE CREAM

The very soft-looking gerbil with either of these color variations sports a coat that is an arresting variation of

*The red-eyed
cream gerbil.*

the agouti. Though he retains the agouti's white or cream-colored underside, his banded agouti coat is lacking the black layer, thus creating a lovely color that is a mixture of the brown and yellow bands remaining on the hair shafts. In the argente golden, this results in a red-eyed, golden appearance that is also referred

to as *cinnamon*. The red-eyed argente cream, on the other hand, also known as a *cinnamon cream,* sports a more apricot-hued coat.

BLACK

A gerbil described as a "black" may be completely black (the eyes are black, as well), as is seen most often

45

in carefully bred show gerbils. The more common black, however, sports some white hairs or even white patches here or there, usually on the gerbil's throat or feet.

The black gerbil.

DOVE/LILAC

Though considered two distinct color variations, dove and lilac gerbils are very similar to each other. Both are gray gerbils, the results of breeding between argente and black gerbils, with the dove gerbil being somewhat lighter in color than the lilac because of an additional infusion of genes from white gerbils.

The red-eyed gray gerbil.

WHITE

There is a variety of white gerbils, all of which share nearly identical appearances, but which are distinctly different in the eyes of geneticists and genetics-savvy gerbil enthusiasts. These gerbils typically include a variety of dark-tailed, pink-eyed white gerbils, the specific names for which change as rapidly as the number of variations. One up-and-coming popular white variation is the silver fox, a white gerbil with black eyes and some black on his back.

The white gerbil.

The white spotted cream gerbil.

SPOTTED/PIED

A gerbil of any color may be considered a spotted gerbil if he sports white spots or blaze-like markings on his head, his neck area, the tip of his tail, and his underside. If those white spots are sprinkled elsewhere through the coat, he is probably a pied instead of a spotted gerbil.

chapter 4

Bringing
Your Gerbils
Home

Once you have decided which gerbils will be best for you, you have to start thinking about what you need to do to welcome these small critters into your household and help them settle in. You know what they say about first impressions: Help ensure your gerbils' first impressions of life within your home are as positive as possible, and you'll make the experience more pleasant for everyone involved.

Be Prepared

Of course we are assuming that you will honestly imagine what life will be like with a pair of gerbils in your home long before you actually bring the little critters into the household—and preferably long before you choose your new pets, too. Then, once you make the decision to welcome these pocket pets into your home, you can get the household ready for them.

Preparing in this way means that you need to get out there and buy all the supplies you'll need: the gerbils' house (aquarium-style tank, cage, etc.) and all the necessary accessories, food, bedding, food and water receptacles, toys, exercise wheel and so forth. Regard the shopping spree to procure all these items as an exciting adventure, your first step toward bringing new living creatures into your home and into your life. It should be exciting. If it's not, and you view it as a drudgery, perhaps it's time to rethink your decision to bring new pets home in the first place.

Once you have your supplies assembled, it's time to get organized. First, choose where your pets will be living—in other words, where their living quarters will be in your home. Remember, gerbils, quiet little animals that they are, don't tolerate noise, stress and rough handling. With this important fact in mind, choose a location for the gerbil abode that is out of the primary lines of household traffic and noise, that is sheltered from direct sunlight or drafts, and that receives normal lighting during the day and is dark at night.

When the animals' arrival is emminent, set up the house to receive its new inhabitants. Your goal is to make it as comfortable as possible for your gerbils. If there are kids in the home, then, by all means, enlist their help in setting up the gerbil habitat, too. This will help to teach them what an important undertaking caring for an animal is and jump-start their investment in the gerbils' care and their compassion for the new family pets. The keeping of pets such as gerbils should be educational as well as enjoyable, so you might as well begin this process even before the gerbils arrive.

Your gerbil is happiest when her home's temperature ranges between 70° and 80°F.

This pre-arrival stage is also a good time to start checking out some local veterinarians to find one with

experience in caring for pocket pets, particularly gerbils. This may be a new concept to you, just as it is even
to many veterinarians. But more and more practitioners
these days are expanding their horizons in the direction
of small and exotic pets in response to the increasing
popularity of these animals in American homes. The
field of veterinary medicine acknowledges that owners
can grow quite attached to these
animals, and when they are ailing,
their keepers are willing to seek
medical help for them.

You can find such veterinarians by
calling offices directly, as well as
asking local animal shelters and
fellow gerbil and small-animal
owners. Within a given area, there
are usually particular veterinarians
who are known for their expertise
in various fields of veterinary
medicine. As you poll people for
the names of skilled pocket pet veterinarians, you
will probably notice that certain names keep
cropping up.

> ## LOCATING YOUR
> ## GERBILS' HOME
>
> The location of your gerbils in your
> home is important for their health
> and well-being. Choose a spot
> that:
>
> • is away from household noise.
>
> • is away from direct sunlight
>   and drafts.
>
> • receives normal daytime light
>   and is dark at night.

Go ahead and call or visit the recommended vet offices
and ask any questions you may have about the care and
health of your new arrivals. You may even want to make
a short appointment to have your new pets examined
for overall health when you first bring them home. A
brief checkup can convince you that, yes, your gerbils
are as healthy as you thought they were. The veterinarian can also confirm for you that both of them really
are females as you had been told—or surprise, surprise, that the little black one is actually a he, not a she.
Better to learn this in the beginning than to find out
with the unexpected arrival of ten new baby gerbils in
your household when you were just getting used to caring for two.

Welcome Home

At last the day arrives, the fateful day when you will
bring your new gerbils home. Their cozy abode is

ready; fresh bedding, food and water await; and you anticipate the arrival of your new pets with excitement.

Before you officially welcome your new little bundles of joy home, you will need a container to transport them. Carefully prepare all of this ahead of time, too, and even the trip home can act as the first step in making your gerbils feel at home—and in earning their trust.

The container should be a secure, ventilated box. Were you bringing a kitten home, one of those cardboard kitten carriers would suffice, but you're bringing rodents home, and cardboard is anything but gnaw-resistant. A heavy plastic box is preferable, perhaps one of those plastic storage containers available at discount department stores, with some small air holes punched into the top.

If you're looking for something a bit more reusable, you might purchase a small plastic-sided rodent cage that is too small to be the gerbils' permanent home, but is ideal for travel and similarly temporary lodging. Another option is a sturdy airline-style carrier made for kittens and very small dogs. Either of these could serve as a hospital or travel cage later on, or a holding cage during gerbil housecleaning time. With the airline carrier, you must, however, guard against the gerbils' escape. A small rodent might be able to squeeze through the wire door and ventilation windows on such a carrier, so it's wise to line these with small mesh screen to make sure you arrive home with the two gerbils you brought from the pet shop or the breeder's house.

Selecting a veterinarian right away can reassure you that your gerbils are happy and healthy.

You should try to make any container you choose as comfortable as possible for the gerbils, so cover the floor of the box or carrier with a layer of fresh bedding

51

(which you purchased ahead of time). You may offer the gerbils a treat or two, perhaps a sunflower seed, to reward them for entering the transportation carrier (even if it wasn't done all that voluntarily), and supply them with a chew toy to nibble on should they feel stress en route to their new home. If the sides of the carrier are transparent, you might also want to furnish the carrier with a small hiding box (either plastic or cardboard), so the gerbils can maintain their comfortable privacy during what may be a rather stressful experience for them.

Speaking of stress, try to imagine this experience through the small bright eyes of your new pets. These

are tiny animals who are being uprooted from all that is familiar to them, all the familiar scents, sounds and surroundings. Granted, this transition is probably easier for a pair of gerbils than it would be for a solitary animal like a hamster, for the ger-

Homeward bound!

bils have each other to turn to for comfort and company, but it's stressful all the same. To ease the stress, keep your voice low—and instruct everyone in the household to do the same. Indeed, try to keep the entire household quiet for a few days to allow the new resident gerbils to settle in.

Once you cross the threshold with the new gerbils, take them directly to their enclosure, release them into the confines of their new home and leave them alone. They need time to take a house tour at their leisure and to figure out what's what and what's where: the bed, the food dish, the water bottle, the hiding boxes, the burrowing potential of the bedding.

Because gerbils rely primarily on their ears and their noses to figure out the world around them, they will revel in this opportunity not only to get acquainted with the physical layout of their new environment, but also with the new scents and sounds around them— and that includes your scent and the sound of your voice. In time, that scent and that voice may become two of the most welcome stimuli in the gerbils' sensory repertoire, stimulants that send them running to the wall of their abode begging to spend time and languish in the attention of their favorite non-gerbil being.

Honor your gerbils' perspective during this critical introduction time—address them with a soft voice and a respectful distance—and you will offer your new pets the smoothest, most pleasant "welcome" they could ask for. Were you fluent in gerbil language, you'd no doubt hear the furry pair softly squeaking their mutual approval of their new caretaker and their new sur- roundings. Earning such approval and, later, the trust that comes with it should be your goal when you decide to bring a gentle gerbil pair into your home and into your life.

Initial Introductions

Of course, you will not be leaving your gerbils com- pletely alone during those first few days, but you are wise to keep your distance, coming into contact only to feed the gerbils, to change the water in the water bot- tle, to rotate the toys and to remove any soiled bedding or uneaten food. Though you will no doubt be proud of your adorable new pets, this is no time to hold a party in their honor—nor is it time to allow the kids to bring a crowd of friends in to meet the newest addi- tions to the family. You're trying to alleviate and pre- vent gerbil stress, not cause and amplify it.

It may be tough—it's hard to resist those soft, cute, furry physiques, those tiny paws and the twitchy, curi- ous noses, but resist you must. Now is not the time to cuddle and play, but you will be rewarded for your patience. Remember, good things come to those who wait.

When you decide the waiting period is over— depending on the individual gerbils, after only a few hours, or even after a day or two—you can venture forth to say hi. Again, you must resist the urge to thrust your hand into the enclosure and grab a gerbil. No, no, no. Instead, try a more gradual approach.

For that initial introduction, make sure the room is quiet and peaceful and place your hand in the gerbil house. Keep it very still, very relaxed. If you want, place a small treat in your palm to help sweeten the deal. As naturally curious as many gerbils tend to be, they won't be able to help but come forward and inspect. It may be one gerbil, it may be both, but once they do venture forward, continue to hold your hand still, and evaluate the situation to decide what to do next.

If you wish to take an extremely gradual approach—and there's nothing wrong with that, even if the gerbils seem relaxed and curious—you may want to retract your hand, secure the door to the gerbil house and repeat the same exercise a short time later. If the gerbils seemed frightened of you upon that first meeting, then you have no choice but to be patient if you wish to start out on firm footing with these animals. Either way, with your gentle approach, the gerbils should

*Allow new
gerbils time to
explore their
new home before
handling them.*

grow accustomed to having your hand and its attendant scent within their territory, and grow to trust what is familiar. That trust ultimately should manifest in a desire to explore further.

Whether you wait or, because of the gerbils' enthusiastic welcome, wish to proceed to the next step upon the initial introduction, eventually you will want to encourage them to hop up on your hand. Entice your gerbils with a treat resting in your palm or a slight and very gentle tap on the their rear ends. As many a gerbil owner has discovered, you many need to provide no encouragement at all. The gerbils' curiosity and their growing trust in their caretaker could lead them up there naturally, perhaps within hours of joining their new family.

There will surely come a moment during these dances of introduction when you will feel your gerbils' teeth on your skin. Don't be alarmed. This is the gerbils' way of getting to know you. They may even be attempting to groom you, just as gerbils groom each other as part of their communal bonding activities. There is a big difference between this friendly nibble and an outright bite that breaks the skin, the latter of which is a rare response from a gerbil. Just pay attention and see how the gerbils are responding to the presence of your hand nearby. And respect what they have to tell you.

Finally, when you think the moment is right, you can reach in and pick up one of your gerbils. Assuming you have done your groundwork gradually and quietly, this moment can be as exciting for the gerbil as it is for you.

> **GAINING YOUR GERBILS' TRUST**
>
> The most important element in gaining the trust of your gerbils is patience. Allow your new pets to get accustomed to you at their own pace. Introduce your hand slowly and in a relaxed way. Let the gerbils come to you. A small treat in the palm of your hand can induce curiosity and help strengthen the bond between you and your gerbils. If they don't investigate right away, be patient and try again later.

You may want to initiate this next step in gerbil caretaking by first picking up whom you perceive as the dominant member of the resident pair, an act that may inspire the more submissive animal to follow suit more easily. When the time is right, look around the room, and make sure it is free of escape hatches (open sliding glass doors), curious dogs or cats (also known as gerbil predators), and anything else that might present a danger should you drop the small animal and find yourself faced with the challenge of rescuing an escaped, and possibly frightened, gerbil.

Careful Handling

Small as she is, and as potentially wiggly as she is, a gerbil must be picked up and handled very securely, but also very gently, which is why the trust element is so crucial.

Before we get into the specifics of how to pick up and hold a gerbil, it is important to state uncategorically that you must never, ever, *ever* pick up or hold a gerbil by her tail. Don't even think about it. That long furry tail was not placed at the back end of the gerbil's cute, stocky little body as a handle. Pulling on the tail or yanking on it in any way not only risks great injury, damage and pain to your pet, but also risks your losing her trust and respect. Breach the "no holding by the tail" contract, and the gerbil isn't likely to welcome the presence of your hand near her for a long time, even if

your hand is nowhere near her tail. So, learn the proper way to handle your gerbil and insist that anyone else who will have contact with your pet—especially children and unruly teenagers—do the same. Period.

Now that the critical tail point has been made, we move on to how you *should* handle this small animal. A gerbil should be picked up and carried with two hands that

Always hold your gerbil with great care and never by the tail.

are held in a cup-like position, both to protect her and to offer her a sense of security. First, gently work one hand under the gerbil so you can support the gerbil's small body in your palm. As you begin to lift the gerbil up and off the secure footing of her enclosure, cup your other hand over her back so she is held securely both underneath and above her small frame.

If you have overestimated your gerbil's sense of security, and she starts to squirm, whatever you do, don't squeeze her. When you're first gauging her reaction to being handled, pick her up only above surfaces where a fall will not result in pain or broken bones—for example, over the bedding of her enclosure or a pillow on the couch. In most cases, though, a tight, reflexive squeeze from your hands could do more damage to your gerbil than accidentally dropping her.

It's wise to keep early handling sessions short so everyone can get accustomed to the experience—and always make sure they occur in a room that is safe for gerbils (no accessible live electrical cords, no dogs and cats and no unruly children). As a rule, gerbils tend to be rather fun-loving, and in the hands of those they trust, many will learn to anticipate and even beg for time spent out of the gerbil house with their owners.

Before you know it, your daily routine may include gently lifting your gerbil out of her cage and then giggling as she shimmies up your arm for her favorite perch on your shoulder (a propensity she shares with the rat). As you sit contentedly in a chair while thumbing through a magazine, with a soft little gerbil perched in equal contentment on your shoulder, perhaps nibbling at your ear-

Soon you can enjoy a warm relationship with your gerbil.

lobe and grooming a stray hair or two, you'll think back and be grateful that you remained patient while getting to know your animal. That gentle little gerbil perched atop your shoulder is your reward—and the trust she has in you is hers.

New Responsibilities, New Routines

Part of getting acquainted with your new gerbil pets is adjusting to your new routine and all the responsibilities involved when you take on the care of new animal companions. Though gerbils, like most rodents, are notoriously easy to take care of, too many people make the mistake of underestimating the amount of care they *do* require. And as you have seen, the gerbil isn't one to complain, but she can suffer.

Gerbils require regular attention for both their emotional and physical well-being. Gerbils, like virtually every pet species, thrive on a routine. To ensure that you get off on the right foot, get started with the new routine right away. Instituting the routine from day one will not only help you get accustomed to what is required of you now as the caretaker of these small animals, but it will also help the gerbils get accustomed to what they may expect from their new owners. Gerbils who understand when you will care for them each day are far more likely to live in comfort and contentment. It's part of the all-important trust issue. With standard, routine care, the energies of gerbils who trust their owners will be directed toward enjoying the people in their lives rather than worrying about how they will be treated from one day to the next.

Your gerbil enclosure will periodically need to be thoroughly cleaned.

Every day you will need to feed the gerbils, remove soiled bedding and uneaten food and check the animals for any signs that could indicate health problems, such as diarrhea or dampness on a gerbil's rear end, a lack of appetite or listless behavior. It's also wise to wash the food dish and the water bottle every day to

help keep your pets healthy and the premises as sanitary and odorless as possible.

And while we're on the subject of cleaning, you will also need to do a wholesale cleaning of the gerbil house periodically, which means removing old bedding completely and replacing it, and scrubbing the walls and furnishings. Depending on the individual habits of the gerbils, and the individual dedication of their owners, this may be done anywhere from once every week to once every month. As a rule, gerbils do not require complete housecleaning as frequently as do some rodent pets, as gerbils don't tend to produce as much odor as some of their rodent brethren. This advantage is especially true if you keep up daily maintenance, which should be part of your new routine, since it is part of the responsibility you take on when you decide to bring gerbil pets into your home.

chapter 5

Housing
Your
Gerbils

Every gerbil must have a home, of course, and that home must be properly designed, cleaned and maintained. A gerbil's home is his castle, his haven, his sanctuary. It is where he can retreat from the noises and odd goings-on of the large two-legged creatures with whom he

lives. Your job, then, is to create that haven and to ensure it satisfies both his emotional and physical needs.

What follows is a discussion of the various housing options available for gerbils, the pros and cons of each, and how they can be maintained for the gerbils' benefit. No matter what you choose, remain ever mindful of the safety of your tiny pets and their well-being within a human household.

59

Wire, Glass and Tubes: Traditional Gerbil Housing Options

There are three "traditional" options for housing gerbils, including the wire cage, the glass aquarium modified for gerbil residents, and the tube set-ups designed to simulate the underground burrows and tunnels in which many rodent species reside in the wild. Let's examine each one and see what it can add to, or detract from, a gerbil's life experience. And remember, regardless of which housing type you choose, set it up in a quiet corner of the house, out of the direct line of household traffic and sheltered from drafts or direct sunlight—noise and extreme heat and cold are all detrimental to a gerbil's health and well-being.

THE WIRE CAGE

Once upon a time rodent pets were automatically placed in cages, no questions asked. But through the years, a desire to provide such animals with conditions that permit them to follow more closely their instincts within a captive environment has emerged among pet owners. When we speak of a small, burrowing animal like the gerbil, then, the cage may not be the ideal home, especially if you intend to supply your pets with a nice thick layer of bedding into which they may burrow. All you need to do is consider the potential mess—metal bars aren't all that efficient when you're trying to hold wood shavings or corncob bedding material within a confined space.

The primary benefit of the wire cage is that it provides ample ventilation to the resident animals, though this may be more crucial to other rodent species, as gerbils are not as prone to respiratory problems as their brethren. Another advantage is that several wire cages can be linked together if you wish to create your own custom caging system for your pets, stacking several wire cages on top of each other or beside each other in a makeshift replica of the gerbils' classic underground system. (Undertaking this project, however, is rather complicated and can endanger the resident gerbils' safety if you're not careful or aren't quite sure what you're doing.) If you do wish to house your gerbils in a wire cage, make sure the door can be securely closed and locked, that it has a solid, non-wire bottom (to protect the feet), and that the bars are close enough together to prevent escape or injury.

Indeed, injury is a great concern for gerbils in a wire cage. A cage made of cheap-grade metal can rust; exposed wires or similarly rough edges can cause cuts and abrasions; the bars can injure the noses of curious gerbil inhabitants; and the resident gerbils may decide to gnaw on the metal, which is not the ideal material for the honing of gerbil teeth. So if the wire cage is your first choice, get one that is made from high-grade stainless steel with high-quality doors and locks—and avoid cages with wood trim that will quickly fall victim to the gerbils' gnawing impulses. Finally, check it periodically for safety-related problems.

An aquarium provides ease of observation and is a good container for gerbil bedding materials.

THE AQUARIUM

Were you to poll the world's gerbil experts, it's a safe bet the majority of them would cite the glass aquarium as your best option for gerbil housing. And they would have plenty of reasons to support their position.

First, the glass aquarium is not only readily available and inexpensive, but it is also the ideal receptacle for a thick layer of bedding into which gerbils so love to dig and burrow. At naptime and bedtime, these critters are happiest when cuddled up together in the sleeping corner of their abode, intertwined to the point where you can't tell where one gerbil ends and the other begins. Safe, clean, aquarium-style housing facilitates such sleeping habits, which can in turn result in happier, more contented gerbils. The aquarium is also easy

61

to clean and provides an unobstructed view of the resident gerbils to external admirers, if the gerbils decide they wish to be viewed at a given time.

The two drawbacks to this seemingly flawless housing choice are the ventilation issue and the escape issue, both of which are linked to the type of top you keep on the aquarium.

To address these potential problems, you simply *must* ensure that your gerbils' aquarium home is fitted with a sturdy, wire mesh top that can be attached securely to the top of the aquarium. While the wide-open-top design of the aquarium offers you easy access to your gerbils and to all the items and materials within the enclosure that require regular maintenance, it must be securely closed when you have finished with such activities.

The screen top provides ventilation, and it also keeps the gerbils safely confined. Gerbils, remember, are jumpers, and many an owner has learned the hard way just how high they can jump when they feel like it—hence the gerbil's reputation as an escape artist. Even if you give your gerbils no reason to want to escape, or even to consider the prospect, sometimes that legendary gerbil curiosity just gets the best of them.

Gerbils are legendary jumpers, so don't tempt fate.

Therefore, you need to protect your pets from the consequences of such impulses.

If you decide the aquarium is the housing choice you wish to provide for gerbils, you will need to get an aquarium that is large enough to prevent a case of cabin fever among the residents. For a pair of gerbils, the ideal-sized gerbil family for beginners, the "right size" translates to a 10- to 20-gallon tank. If you'll be keeping three or four gerbils, the tank size must increase accordingly to at least a 20- to 30-gallon size and so on. Given the reproductive habits of gerbils, if you allow your pets to procreate without restriction, you will soon find yourself with a gerbil population explosion on your hands, and some new aquarium purchases will be in order. Though gerbils in their natural state enjoy extended family life, keeping them all under one roof is not typically possible for the long term. Even in the wild, the families eventually have to branch out.

If, like most owners, your intent is to begin with two gerbils (a same-gender pair, of course) and remain with two gerbils, then stick with the 10- to 20-gallon tank and rest easy. This will provide your pets with ample, easy-to-clean space complete with a thick layer of bedding for sleeping and snuggling, and it will provide you with easy accessibility to and a clear view of your pets.

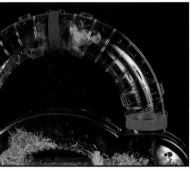

TUBE SET-UPS

Some years back when tube set-up housing for rodent pets became commercially available, they were quite the rage. Here you had a housing situation that mimicked an underground animal's natural inclination to dig great mazes of tunnels and burrows. This contraption was made of clear plastic that permitted owners to peek in and watch their pets scurry and scamper, enjoying a grand old time as they traversed their convoluted home from one end to the other.

Tube systems can provide entertaining views of gerbils, but with long-term use, the plastic is prone to odors and gnawing.

But time and experience have since led a large contingent of keepers of rodents, gerbils and otherwise, to claim that tube set-ups are probably not the ideal housing situation for small rodent pets. Those plastic sides do not withstand the almost supernatural gnawing abilities of rodents all that well, and they seem to collect and intensify odors at a rate and magnitude that most rodent caretakers don't care to have lingering within their homes.

We need not dismiss the tube environment altogether, however. Although it may not be the optimum housing choice for gerbils, it can act as a great accessory for external play. Regard it as a gerbil playground and invite your pets to scamper to their hearts' content during playtime. In this role, the tube set-up won't be your gerbils' primary residence, but it can remain a fun and convenient accessory for you as well as them. It can be quickly and easily cleaned at your convenience, and your gerbils probably won't be inside it long enough to do great damage to the plastic tubing with their teeth.

Natural Group Housing

One more housing option some gerbil owners have explored is natural group housing in an aquarium filled with dirt. Such an arrangement is designed to simulate the way gerbils live in the wild, but be aware that it is a method best left to more experienced gerbil keepers.

This method involves filling an aquarium of at least 20 gallons approximately halfway with parasite- and pesticide-free dirt, peat or straw, packed and arranged to prevent cave-ins. The gerbils are released into their environment, and their natural instincts set in. They will, of course, be fed by external hands, and their keepers should supply them periodically with wood and paper for chewing and making beds, but otherwise they are, for all practical purposes, on their own. They will probably begin to dig their customary tunnels right away, designating individual areas and "rooms" for such distinct purposes as eating, sleeping and eliminating. And, probably in no time, assuming this is a multi-gender domicile, they will begin to populate those areas and rooms. Indeed, this is why natural housing is best suited to experienced types.

The benefit of natural housing is just that—it mimics the "natural" lifestyle the gerbils would be leading in the wild. Some believe it also reduces the incidence of what is called "stereotyped digging" in gerbils, in which the animals dig compulsively in the corners of their enclosure. But this method has significant drawbacks, as well, especially as far as the very nature of pet keeping goes. For example, this arrangement, because it is does mimic nature, can be far dirtier for the pet keeper in terms of upkeep. Uneaten food scattered about can spoil if unseen by the person whose job it is to keep the premises clean and sanitary.

Experienced gerbil owners sometimes opt for natural housing to keep their pets.

If you opt for natural housing, you also may never know exactly how many gerbils you have at a time, since some—especially newborns and other youngsters—may be hidden much, if not all, of the time. And if one of those gerbils happens to die, which will certainly happen from time to time in so large and sprawling a population, the only way you may discover this is when you notice an unpleasant aroma emanating from the gerbil habitat, but you may be unable to locate the unfortunate source of that aroma. You also may never notice when one of your pets begins to show signs of injury or illness; you thus miss the opportunity to get him medical help—and perhaps to save the entire group from a contagious disease.

Indeed, your inability to see your pets is probably the greatest drawback of all with this method. While more traditional housing methods require that you provide your pets with hiding/nest boxes and bedding for burrowing, the natural housing method takes that concept to the extreme. In doing so, it also places a significant, though natural, barrier between gerbils and caretaker, both visually and emotionally.

65

Most people choose gerbils as pets because they enjoy their sweet, gentle temperaments and fascinating social lives and activities. Gerbils housed in an underground, secretive, even mysterious, natural group arrangement may not be as inclined to pay much attention to those who care for them, and you may miss out on much of the fun that gerbils can bring into our lives. It's a shame to think you might miss watching your pets' antics and social interactions, not to mention experiencing the fun you can have with them yourself during gerbil playtime. We might also question the wisdom of potentially increasing the odor within the habitat of an animal that is otherwise renowned as a pet of very little, if any, odor.

If it's a scientific experiment you're looking for, then by all means consider the natural, essentially underground, commune method of gerbil keeping. But if you crave a more hands-on life with a sweet, potentially playful and interactive little creature, one of the more traditional housing methods will better facilitate that relationship. Even though this arrangement may seem more synthetic when compared to a more natural setting, you can still provide your pets with comfortable habitat accessories and design elements that will amply satisfy their natural gerbil instincts and inclinations.

Safe Bedding, Safe Furnishings, Safe Housing

Whether you choose an aquarium enclosure or a wire cage for your gerbils' home, you must provide them with bedding, and the bedding must be safe. You see, not every bedding type is safe for small rodents. The safest bedding options for gerbils (and most rodent pets) include aspen wood shavings, corncob bedding, non-wood cellulose-based products, or paper bedding products. Avoid cedar and pine, which are heavy in oils and dust that can irritate the systems of small animals, often fatally. Avoid, too, fabrics and cloth, especially fluffy fleece material, which may seem cozy to the touch, but which can cause severe internal problems to the unsuspecting gerbil who happens to ingest some of it.

Most gerbils will do their own part in keeping odor at bay within their domicile. They typically designate a specific area of the cage as their bathroom, so that will make your latrine duties simpler. You can further help by arranging your gerbils' home from the beginning with the hiding and nest boxes in one area, food and water in another and toys in yet another. The gerbils in turn will determine where the bathroom is, typically in an area some distance from the sleeping and dining areas.

USE CAUTION WHEN SELECTING GERBIL BEDDING
Cedar and pine are heavy in oils and dust that can be fatal to gerbils. Fabrics and cloth, too, can cause internal problems for your rodent pet. Instead, use aspen wood shavings, corncob bedding, non-wood cellulose-based products or paper bedding products.

You can also tend to your pets' safety and well-being by conducting periodic hazard checks. Examine wire cages for exposed wires and other sharp edges that could cause injury, and make sure the door and locking mechanisms remain in good operating order. Check for similar sharp edges within an aquarium enclosure, and make sure the screen top remains secure and free of rips or tears that might invite a potentially injurious gerbil escape.

Monitor the furnishings within the gerbils' home, as well. First, you will want to supply your pets with toys, the bulk of which will consist of safe chewing items, such as commercially available rodent chew toys and perhaps a pesticide-free limb from a fruit tree. You will also need to supply your pets with a bed or hiding box of some kind—several, in fact. These may be the commercially manufactured plastic kind or a more humble cardboard box model. Round out the furnishings with tube-like toys they can both chew on and hide in, such as PVC pipe segments, empty toilet paper rolls, and empty cardboard oatmeal cylinders. The more the merrier, as far as gerbils are concerned, for a wide variety of toys will help prevent boredom. Rotate the toys so they can seem new again and again and again, and you continue to prevent boredom.

Sometimes the least expensive toy will be your gerbil's favorite!

Some, if not all, of the items with which you furnish your gerbils' home will ultimately fall into disrepair, primarily because the gerbils just can't resist chewing on them. That's okay. It's all part of keeping rodents as pets. You just need to make sure that the toys you choose are safe and made of materials that will not be toxic to a gnawing rodent. In this regard, natural materials tend to be safer than plastic, as anything a gerbil gnaws could be accidentally ingested. In addition to ensuring gerbil safety through furnishing choice,

inspect the toys and furnishings regularly for sharp edges, inappropriate edibility and similar dangers.

Playing Housekeeper

As we have learned, gerbils are fastidiously clean little creatures, and they thrive best when their caretakers recognize this personality trait of theirs and respond accordingly. In other words, they will be thrilled to have owners who do all they can to keep the gerbil house clean and odor-free.

Because these are gerbils we're talking about, upkeep is a bit simpler than it is for other rodents. Water-efficient gerbils produce little urine, so urine-related odor is kept to a minimum. It is thus not too difficult to keep up with the daily maintenance that will keep the bedding and the atmosphere fresh. All you need do is remove soiled bedding as well as uneaten food every day.

For more thorough cleaning, change the bedding entirely anywhere from once a week to once a month. Frequency depends on how messy your particular little critters are and how dedicated you are to adhering to the daily maintenance routine. Experienced gerbil keepers perform their daily duties and then determine when it's time for wholesale cleaning, based on odor that begins to emanate from the gerbil house. In time, once you get to know your pets and their habits, this schedule, too, will become second nature to you.

Wholesale cleaning involves removing the gerbils from their cozy abode and transferring them to comfortable temporary digs to wait out the procedure. Temporary lodgings can be a spare, usually smaller cage or tank you reserve precisely for this purpose, or perhaps the travel container in which you brought your gerbils home. Regardless of what you choose, the enclosure should be clean, escape-proof, safe and smooth and furnished with a bit of clean bedding, a chew toy or two and perhaps a hiding box—all the comforts of home.

With your gerbils safely confined, you can get to work. Remove the old bedding and then clean the surfaces of the cage or aquarium tank with water and mild soap. Do the same with the feeding dish and water bottle (which you should actually clean, if not every day, then every other day), hiding boxes, beds, toys, the exercise wheel—anything that is a permanent fixture in the cage and still in decent shape (this is also the ideal time to check out

the furnishings and toys and discard anything that is beyond the point of enjoyment or safety). After scrubbing these items, whether it be the aquarium walls or a play ball, rinse them, rinse them and rinse them again. You don't want to leave any soap residue behind that could make the resident gerbils ill.

A travel cage makes an excellent place to keep your gerbils while you clean their permanent home.

When It's Time to Travel

It's tough to have to leave your pets behind when you need to leave town, but, in all honesty, that is precisely how gerbils prefer it. Homebodies that they are, they really don't care to be uprooted from their familiar surroundings, sounds and scents to be carted off to some strange and potentially frightening place. A much kinder tactic is to leave the gerbils at home in the cozy abode that you have created for them.

If you will be gone for only a weekend, you can in good
conscience fluff up the gerbils' bedding; leave them an
ample amount of spoil-proof food (seed mix and lab
blocks are good choices); fill the water bottle with
fresh water and hang a second water bottle, as well, just

in case the tube on the
first becomes clogged;
and your pets should
be just fine. There's a
reason gerbils are con-
sidered such easy-care
pets.

If you will be gone for
longer than a week-
end, you may want to
consider enlisting the

*Wooden chew
toys keep gerbils
from getting
bored and allow
them to keep
their teeth in
good shape.*

services of a pet sitter. Gerbils are ideal for such an
arrangement. The pet sitter can come in each day,
remove the soiled bedding, freshen up the food and
water, perhaps offer the gerbils a treat or two, and
make sure that all is well with the little animals. And it
never hurts to remind even skilled pet sitters how critical it is that the screen top or cage door be closed
securely once they have finished caring for your pets.

To locate a pet sitter, you can ask local veterinarians
and animal-shelter staff members for recommenda-
tions. Ask other pet owners, too. When you make contact with someone—preferably someone who is
licensed and bonded for your protection—meet him
or her at your home, introduce your pets and ask any
questions you might have. Once you find someone you
trust, you can relax in knowing that while you are away,
your pets will fare just fine, and you can look forward
to the reunion upon your return.

chapter 6

Feeding
Your
Gerbils

A gerbil's got to eat, and a gerbil owner's got to know how to feed her. In keeping with their species' easy-care reputation, gerbils are quite easy to feed, and, in fact, their health depends on their care-takers' sticking to the simple, natural formula. Read on—you'll see just how easy and how simple that formula is.

Nutritional ABCs

Though the gerbil diet is simple, its complexity lies in its balance. Gerbils, like all mammals and all rodents, require a mix of nutrients if they are to be properly nourished.

In the wild, gerbils collected their balanced mix of nutrients naturally through their daily forages for food, which was often scarce.

As is the case for most rodents, they took what they could get, from seeds to insects, and in the process evolved into creatures that were both hardy and diverse in constitution and in diet.

Contemporary pet gerbils need not hunt for their dinners in such a way, yet their nutritional needs have not changed. Before we delve into how to supply your gerbils with the proper balance of nutrients that is vital to their health, well-being and longevity, let's take a look

at the nutrients themselves and see why and how each plays so important a role.

WATER

Contrary to what some believe, you must supply your gerbils with water each and every day. This may seem like a rather odd, certainly obvious comment to make, but misconceptions abound regarding the gerbil's need for water, one of the world's most important nutrients and the primary component of the gerbil's body.

Hailing from an arid land where water is scarce, gerbils are indeed phenomenally efficient in their

The gerbil conserves water efficiently, but she still requires fresh and ample supplies daily.

absorption of water. Their bodies conserve what little water they can find both from actual water sources and from the vegetation that comprises the majority of their natural diet. As a result, a common fallacy is that, because of the gerbil's background, she can absorb all the water she needs from vegetation she is offered as part of her daily food rations. Wrong! The pet gerbil absolutely must have an ample supply of fresh, clean water offered every single day. Period.

Without this all-important nutrient, gerbils will indeed absorb some moisture from their diet, assuming you supplement their seed mixtures and lab blocks with fresh fruits and vegetables, but it's not enough.

Without proper hydration, their health will suffer dramatically, as will the sweetness of their temperaments, and their lives will be shortened significantly—all because someone believed that gerbils don't need to be offered water as part of their daily rations.

PROTEINS

As the primary building blocks of some of the body's most critical structural tissues—blood, bone, muscle and hair—proteins are obviously necessary nutrients. Once ingested, proteins are broken down into amino acids, which then go on to perform their assigned tasks.

Though in the wild gerbils will sometimes ingest proteins from insects they happen to find while foraging for food, proteins also are available in the vegetable-based items that comprise the bulk of the classic gerbil diet, both of gerbils in the wild and those in captivity. Proteins exist in many of the seeds that comprise the various prepared rodent diets, and in certain vegetables, such as broccoli, that may be offered to a pet gerbil as dietary supplements.

Juicy veggies make healthy treats, but they can't replace water.

FATS AND CARBOHYDRATES

Active little creatures that they are, gerbils require energy to fuel their many daily activities. They receive this energy primarily from the fats and carbohydrates in their diet.

Carbohydrates, which are essentially sugars in nutritional form, are the primary source of energy. Those sugars break down easily and are quickly converted to fuel. Gerbils receive carbohydrates from the seeds and grains in their diet, but an overabundance of carbohydrates that exceeds a gerbil's energy needs can result in an overweight animal.

73

Caring for
Your Gerbils

While pet gerbils are by nature less active than their wild counterparts, and thus more prone to obesity, some fat is nevertheless a must in their diet. In addition to rounding out a gerbil's energy supply, fats also work to insulate the small animal from the cold, play important roles in the absorption of fat-soluble vitamins and assist in proper organ function. Many of the seeds that a gerbil enjoys—particularly her beloved sunflower seeds—are rich in fat, so they should be offered in moderation.

VITAMINS AND MINERALS

Vitamins and minerals are also critical components of the gerbil diet, performing a variety of duties required for proper cell and organ function. Fortunately, these nutrients are typically available in the various foods that comprise the classic gerbil diet. Seeds, grains, fruits, vegetables: All can supply your gerbils with the vitamin and mineral components they require.

We now come to the subject of supplementation. Too often, we assume that if some is good, more must be better. We thus enhance our own diets or those of our pets with an overabundance of vitamin and mineral supplements. The results for gerbils can be identical to the results that occur in our own systems: too many vitamins and minerals, and a disruption to the fine balance that exists between them.

Vitamins and minerals typically work together to perform their functions, so over-supplementation can damage that fine balance by throwing it off kilter. In addition, some vitamins are fat-soluble, meaning that excess cannot be flushed from the body as happens with water-soluble vitamins. Over-supplementation can thus cause health problems itself. While there are conditions that call for supplementation of specific vitamins and minerals—which are readily available in both powder and liquid forms so they may be mixed into the gerbils' food—exercise moderation both in frequency and in amount of supplementation for the sake of your pets' overall health, and proceed under your veterinarian's direction.

What to Feed Your Gerbils

Now that we have discovered what your gerbils need to thrive—a diet rich in variety to ensure nutritional balance—just what should you feed your pets to make sure they receive all they need to satisfy that balance? The answer is easy, especially because experts have studied rodent nutrition and designed foods that target their specific needs. This is thanks, no doubt, to the countless generations of laboratory animals who have inspired nutritional research designed to ensure they survive their experiments.

While we may not care for the roots of the revolution in rodent dietary research, for the good of our pets we can at least be pleased with the subsequent variety of commercial foods now available for the sustenance of small animals. Times have changed dramatically where the feeding of small pets is concerned. Perhaps they can thank their captive laboratory predecessors for their sacrifices.

While even experts may disagree on what might be considered the "ideal" gerbil diet, most agree that the basis of that diet should be one or more of the following items. The first is a fresh and healthy *seed mix* (light on the sunflower seeds, please, which are quite fattening).

GERBILS' NUTRITIONAL NEEDS

Like humans, gerbils require a variety of food that provides balanced nutrition. Gerbil owners must be attentive to their pets' intake of:

- water.

- protein.

- fats and carbohydrates.

- vitamins and minerals.

The goal is to offer a seed mix with as wide a variety of ingredients as possible. Experienced gerbil keepers have even been known to blend their own seed mixes from several types of bird seed mixes to cut down costs and to ensure that their pets receive a variety of seeds, grains and other specific ingredients they wish to offer.

Next on the list are *lab blocks,* which are, as their name implies, complete and balanced "blocks" that you can leave in the gerbil house without worrying about spoilage. These are a favorite among many rodent

75

owners because of the blocks' convenience and nutritional value. Lab blocks are also the ideal security ration when you must leave your gerbils alone for the weekend and want to make sure that they have plenty of fresh food while you are away.

Finally, we have *pellets,* which, like lab blocks, are another processed, multi-nutrient food for rodents. Pellets usually are not as highly regarded as lab blocks, however, because they don't tend to be quite as "complete and balanced" as lab blocks. You may, however, bypass this shortcoming by feeding pellets in conjunction with another type of high-quality food.

Indeed, many a seasoned gerbil keeper recommends feeding gerbils a combination of commercially pre-pared foods to facilitate nutritional balance and to offer the gerbil some variety. Two popular combina-tions are a fresh, high-quality seed mix coupled with lab blocks, or that same high-quality seed mix com-bined with a pellet product high in vitamins and min-erals. Some owners also round out the nutritional components by offering their pets an insect or meal-worm from time to time for a bit of extra protein, but squeamish owners will be relieved to hear that this is not at all necessary, and gerbil keepers who do it are in the minority.

While these commercial products comprise the foun-dation of the gerbils' diet, you may supplement them with a moderate helping of fresh veggies and occa-sionally fruits—broccoli, hay and apple are a few choices—and perhaps a sprig of dandelion greens from time to time. Wash these items thoroughly, and choose fresh foods that are free of pesticides, which can be toxic to gerbils.

As for other items that should remain off-limits to ger-bils, these include sweets that we humans so adore (cake, candy and so forth), foods grown from bulbs rather than seeds, foods that are less than fresh and anything contaminated by pesticides. The main ingredients of the healthy gerbil diet are simple and readily available. Don't complicate things by adding ingredients that your pets neither need nor can afford in terms of health and vitality.

Finally, serve your gerbils' meals with ample supplies of fresh, clean water, no matter how many vegetables and fruits your pets may be eating. Gerbils need food and they need water—and you need to supply them with both every day.

How to Feed Your Gerbils

There is a philosophy circulating out there that holds the best way to feed gerbils is to simulate their wild lifestyles by throwing a handful of gerbil food on the floor of the gerbil house and letting them forage for the morsels. Experts, however, disagree, believing this method just causes mess and odor as food becomes buried in the bedding where it may spoil unseen. In addition, "foraging" in this way doesn't really mimic the act of gerbil foraging in the wild, so what's the point?

A better method for feeding gerbils, and one that won't drive you crazy, is to place the food in a low-sided dish, one approximately the shape and size of a tuna can. You may want to use one dish for the seed mix and a separate one for fresh veggies. The best dishes are made of gnaw-resistant ceramic with a heavy bottom that cannot be easily tipped over, thus avoiding the aforementioned throw-the-food-on-the-floor-and-let-it-spoil method. As for your pets' water, serve this in a traditional water bottle with a drinking tube. Place the water in a dish, and, for obvious reasons, you'll have a mess on your hands. Just imagine all that nice fresh bedding suddenly soaked with water, and you'll understand. Given their background in an arid land, gerbils don't do well in a humid environment; wet bedding and subsequent moisture in the air are not an ideal situation.

Feed your gerbil a variety of seeds, lab blocks and pellets.

Caring for
Your Gerbils

Feed your gerbils once a day, a meal consisting of, say, a dish of seed mix, a helping of lab blocks and a small serving of fresh vegetables. It doesn't really matter when you do this, as long as you stick to a routine. The challenge is to prevent your gerbils from becoming fixated on a specific type of food. It's not unusual, for example, for a gerbil to pick all the sunflower seeds from a seed mix and then wait patiently for you to offer more. This is why you should offer a variety (and make sure there are not too many sunflower seeds in the seed mix), so the gerbil learns to dine on a variety of foods and thus take in a full complement of nutrients.

Each day you should also remove the uneaten food. For example, if you feed the gerbils in the morning, remove the uneaten food, particularly the fresh food, in the late afternoon or evening (you may leave lab blocks, as these are not prone to quick spoilage and can serve as a snack should the gerbils get hungry later on). It's not unusual for the gerbils to eat all their seed mix, but if some is left, remove the leftovers before placing a fresh serving in the dish the next day.

Include a small serving of vegetables in your gerbil's daily diet.

Your mission is not only to make sure your gerbils ingest a balanced component of nutrients each day, but also that the nutrients they receive come from the freshest of foods. Never feed old or spoiled foods, which aren't good for gerbils just as they aren't good

for humans. Finally, to ensure that your gerbils always receive the freshest rations, resist the temptation to purchase mass quantities of seed mix or pellets in bulk because of a discounted cost. If you are the caretaker of only a pair of gerbils, or even two pairs, bulk food can spoil or at least deteriorate in the quality of its nutrients. Smaller supplies stored in airtight containers will better serve your pets, and perhaps lead to healthier and longer lives.

78

How to Treat Your Gerbils

Every once in a while it's fun to offer your gerbils a treat, perhaps when they are playing with you in a gerbil-proofed family room, or as an enticement when they are learning to run through a maze you have designed for them. And, indeed, it is a delight to watch the reactions of such tiny, adorable animals when they spy a favored treat hidden between your fingers. However, just as you do not want to feed your gerbils in an unhealthy manner, you don't want to offer treats in such a way that will lead to obesity, and treats can easily pave the way to that fate.

An overweight gerbil may indeed find great enjoyment in the act of eating, but she is not a healthy gerbil. Gerbils are not naturally slim, trim and svelte. They are stocky in build, yet muscular and athletic in movement. An overweight gerbil cannot play and jump like a gerbil of proper weight can. She can't snuggle as comfortably with her fellow gerbils or perhaps even gain access to all those hard-to-reach places at grooming time. Even worse, excess weight can obstruct the proper functioning of her organs and eventually lead to a premature, and probably uncomfortable, end.

Offer treats to your gerbil from time to time, but not enough to encourage obesity.

Such a fate is not what any caring gerbil owner wishes for his or her pet, but it will be the unintended result should you allow the fun of overfeeding a gerbil to supersede the animal's health and well-being. The gerbil's metabolic system, sculpted by life in an arid land where food was often scarce, will not tolerate massive servings of rich, fatty foods. You must then commit to a common-sense feeding regimen tailored to the gerbil's simple constitution, and supplement the core diet with sensible treats offered in moderation.

One culprit often implicated in gerbil obesity is the sunflower seed. Many gerbils would do anything for

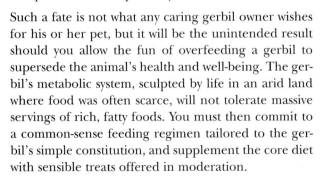

one of these tasty, fat-rich morsels, and if you bow to their requests too frequently, you will find yourself with fat gerbils on your hands. Sunflower seeds may be included in your pets' seed mix (not too many), but they should be offered as treats only on very special occasions.

Other healthy treats include a small slice of dried apricot, a small serving of Cheerios breakfast cereal, a couple of raisins, an apple slice—nothing rich, fatty or prepared by a gourmet. No leftover lasagna or beef Wellington, thank you very much. Keep it simple. Keep it healthy. And remember the commitment you made to maintaining your pets' health and well-being.

Remember, too, that sometimes you can offer your gerbils a treat that really isn't a food at all but will still be appreciated. This could include a clean, slender branch from a pesticide-free fruit tree or new and special chew toys with unique aromas, shapes and textures that are made especially for rodents. Just the unique nature of such items identifies them in the gerbils' minds as "treats." In offering them to your pets, you are offering treats that won't contribute to obesity and will quench the gerbils' curiosity and thirst for something new. At the same time, in

A wooden chew toy may delight your gerbil as much as an edible treat.

satisfying the gerbils' natural chewing impulses, treats of this kind help to hone and maintain the health of the gerbils' teeth. That is certainly superior to a treat that, after offering a momentary gastronomic pleasure, will contribute to the downfall of your pets' health. Your gerbils don't know any better, but you do. Take care of them.

chapter 7

Keeping
Your Gerbils
Healthy

Those who may be ignorant of the gerbil's abundant charms may scoff at the notion of keeping a gerbil healthy. But those who have come under this wee animal's spell know that once a pair of gerbils becomes a fixture within the household, their health and longevity become a very real concern. To address that concern, you must take some time to acquaint yourself with the various conditions that can arise and threaten the health of these special little pets. The  more you know, the better equipped you'll be both to recognize and to prevent these unfortunate occurrences.

Gerbils As Patients

As a rule, gerbils are considered some of the healthiest of the rodent pets. They do not seem to be as easily affected by respiratory infections or diarrhea-related illnesses as some of their rodent brethren. Nevertheless, they can contract illnesses and sustain injuries that require attention.

And just what kind of attention might we be talking about? Well, a couple decades ago, had you uttered the idea that perhaps someone's ailing gerbil should be taken for a visit to the veterinarian, you would have been laughed out of the room. But fortunately for gerbils and the countless other small animal companions out there, times have changed; veterinary science has made leaps and bounds in the care of all animals, and small animals and the people who love them emerge healthier for it.

Your gerbil may require medical attention from time to time.

While gerbil medicine has not reached the heights of, say, canine and feline medicine, we are now better educated both in gerbil care and in the treatment of various problems that can affect these small animals. Veterinarians who have experience in the care of small pets are now available from coast to coast, and even the public at large is accepting the concept of taking a gerbil to the veterinarian. In most cases, these visits are made not for annual booster vaccinations, as there are no vaccines for gerbils, but for consultation when you notice signs of illness or injury in your pet.

We must be honest, though, that ever-lingering is this question: How far should you go with a gerbil's veterinary attention and treatment? Though gerbils are small animals, veterinary bills are not calculated commensurate with the size of the patient, and as cynics are quick to point out, you could buy a whole herd of gerbils for the cost of one veterinary appointment. Now, no one is saying that in the event of illness you must make heroic financial sacrifices to treat a small animal that may or may not survive. But we are honor-bound to help relieve the suffering of an ill or injured gerbil, even if that means choosing humane euthanasia.

In general, the various conditions that affect gerbils are all fairly standard and well-documented, and treatment usually involves the administration of antibiotics either orally or topically. Rarely, then, if ever, should you be asked to deplete your bank account for some extraordinary treatment (and if you are asked, you are well within your rights to decline).

Your gerbil's visit to the vet can include everything from receiving medication to having his nails trimmed.

Assuming you are working with a qualified and experienced veterinarian, you can work together both to diagnose the problem and, if possible, to treat it. If treatment is an option, be prepared for some hands-on participation, as many gerbil health conditions require at-home care.

Preventive Medicine

Of course, where health is concerned, prevention is always the best medicine, and that applies to the health of gerbils just as profoundly as it does to virtually every other species on the planet. While it is wise to find a veterinarian who is well-versed in the care of gerbils in case you ever need such services, the best health insurance you can offer your gerbil pets is a sound care routine with procedures custom-designed to preserve and protect the health of these unique little animals.

Preventive care begins with the gerbils' daily health routine. Keep the bedding clean (and stick to such healthy materials as aspen shavings and corncob or paper bedding products); keep the water fresh within the water bottle (and ignore old wives' tales about gerbils not needing water to drink); and keep the food fresh. And, of course, clean the food and water receptacles daily. Resist that pesky temptation to ply your pets with inappropriate treats or too much food, and stick to a simple, healthy diet throughout your pets' lives. Round this out with a regular dose of affection, gentle handling, an interesting array of appropriate chew toys and an exercise wheel specifically designed for small pets with tails (one with solid sides and no spokes) to prevent tail injuries.

> **GERBIL SAFETY TIP**
>
> An exercise wheel can be an excellent way to encourage gerbil activity. Make sure, however, that you choose a wheel designed with the gerbil tail in mind. It should have solid sides and no spokes.

As for grooming, while this is an important component in keeping pets healthy, for gerbils it's best that they be allowed to carry out this function on their own—on themselves and with each other. Baths really aren't necessary for gerbils, and they may serve only to distress the tiny animals and open them up to illness. Allow them to tend to their grooming responsibilities on their own, and watch for signs that indicate they may not be doing so, such as an unkempt coat, which may be a serious symptom of illness.

You must also remain mindful of the gerbils' potential stress. Stress, as we know, can take a great toll on overall health, and this is very true of tiny animals living among humans. Be sensitive to stress's potential harm and keep the gerbils' home situated in a corner of the house that is quiet, relatively free of traffic and off-limits to the family dog and cat. Make sure this location is also sheltered from drafts, direct sunlight and humidity, all of which can be very dangerous to gerbil health. Prevent anxiety even further by furnishing the gerbils' abode with a selection of enclosed hiding and nest boxes into which they can retreat when the rigors of the outside world become too much for them. Keep an eye, too, on those who visit your home—particularly friends of your kids, who may be fascinated by the presence of gerbils in the household. All such interactions should be supervised for the gerbils' safety and sanity.

Gerbils also are safer and saner (and more stress-free) when their caretakers remember and honor these small animals' perspective on the world. Do not, for example, throw an unknown third party into a happy and established pair situation. That's just asking for fights (possibly to the death), injuries, potentially life-threatening stress and, to top it all off, perhaps even exposure to an animal that may be carrying a contagious illness. If you think about it, the gerbil's xenophobia has probably protected him from many of the health problems so prevalent in other rodent species. Gerbils prefer to remain only with known entities—no strangers allowed. They're not being rude; they're just protecting themselves.

All these elements, when practiced diligently and consistently,

The presence of cats and other curious animals can cause great stress in gerbils.

are powerful medicine in the protection of your pet gerbils' health. Gerbils blessed with such responsible long-term care have a much better chance of reaching the upper limits of their species' life span—and enjoying the journey along the way.

Signs of an Ailing Gerbil

When you are deeply involved in the daily care of gerbils—or any pets—you are in a far better position to recognize signs of trouble than you would be if you never took the time to get to know them through the daily care regimen. Sometimes these signs are quite obvious—for example, when blood is involved. But sometimes they are far more subtle, as when a gerbil who typically adores raisins turns his nose up at your offer of this favored morsel. Only if you know your gerbil and his habits well will you recognize this seemingly inconsequential latter response as the potentially serious sign of illness it may be. And, as is the case with most pets (and people, too), the earlier treatment is sought, the better and easier the chance the animal has of recovering, or at least of avoiding pain and suffering.

It is thus in your gerbils' best interests that you get to know your pets well and pay attention to the maintenance of their condition. Get acquainted with their habits, as well. Any change in physical condition or behavior could be that initial sign that will ensure your pets receive quick treatment and, we hope, a speedy recovery.

What follows then are the classic signs of an ailing gerbil. Watch for them and take them seriously:

- Loss of appetite or sudden disinterest in a favorite treat

- Diarrhea or a wet rear end

- Limping or similarly awkward or difficult movement

- Listlessness, depression, lethargy

- Labored breathing or breathing with a clicking sound

- Lumps or bumps, particularly on or around the scent gland on the underside of the gerbil's body

- An unkempt coat or a gerbil's refusal to groom himself

- Blood

- Clumsy lopsided walking or a head tilt (possible ear infection or injury)

- Drooling (possible overgrown teeth or a misaligned jaw)

- Excessive scratching (possible parasites or reaction to unsanitary living conditions)

Common Gerbil Injuries

While gerbils are essentially very healthy animals, they are not immune from the freak accidents and other dangers that can lurk around the corner during their daily lives. The following are some of the more common injuries that can affect gerbils and, when possible, how they might be treated and prevented.

CUTS AND ABSCESSES

Should you notice blood on your gerbil's body, the cause is usually a minor cut that was in turn caused by a fight with a cagemate or a run-in with a sharp surface in the gerbil house (a rather common occurrence in wire cages). Treatment usually involves cleansing the site and applying antibiotic ointment to prevent infection.

If, however, the wound becomes an abscess, which is most common with puncture wounds, the situation is a bit more serious and painful. Abscesses are typically the result of gerbil fights, but they are also common within a gerbil's mouth. In time you may notice a discharge and foul odor from the wound—a definite sign of infection—which will require cleansing (if the gerbil will tolerate it) and the administration of antibiotics. This is one situation—a painful one, at that—where consultation with the veterinarian is advised.

The presence of blood on the mouth or elsewhere may indicate an abscess and should be checked by a veterinarian.

BROKEN TAIL

Gerbils, like many of their rodent pet brethren, tend to be big fans of the exercise wheel for expending excess energy, but such sessions can lead to broken gerbil tails. Broken tails can also result when the tail becomes entangled in cage bars or something similarly dangerous in the gerbil house, or, heaven forbid, when a gerbil is held by his tail.

A broken tail can be quite painful for the gerbil and rather gruesome for the gerbil's owner. The break typically leaves the tail bone exposed, which you must treat with a topical antibiotic ointment. From then on, do what you can to keep bedding and food from sticking to the wound, and call the veterinarian should you

suspect infection. In time, the tail will heal, leaving in
its wake either a gerbil with a crooked tail or, if the broken section falls off, a significantly shortened tail. You
may be able to prevent this injury by housing your gerbils in an aquarium and by providing them with an
exercise wheel specially made for
small animals with tails.

*Gerbils love to
play on exercise
wheels.*

BROKEN BONES

There isn't much you can do for a
gerbil with a broken bone, since
casts are not made in so small a
size. All you can really do is make
sure the animal is warm and, if he
has sustained an open compound
fracture, try to apply antibiotic
ointment to prevent infection. If the gerbil is eating,
that is a good sign.

If the break is on a leg, then the gerbil will probably
recover and be up and bouncing around in a few days.
In some cases, especially with open leg breaks that
become infected, the veterinarian may be able to ampu-
tate, but that is a personal choice. Should you make
that choice and the gerbil recovers, he will do fine as a
three-legged gerbil. Nevertheless, sometimes there is
nothing that can be done, and you may need to resort
to euthanasia to end the small animal's suffering.

BLOODY OR RED NOSE

A gerbil's bloody nose typically looks worse that it is.
The most common cause of a bloody nose is an allergy
to the bedding material. If you are not already using
aspen shavings, then make the switch. If you are using
aspen, then try one of the other bedding alternatives,
such as corncob bedding, wood-free cellulose products
or even plain shredded paper. While a veterinary visit
is usually unnecessary for this condition, the doctor
may prescribe an antibiotic to prevent infection.

Sometimes, however, the cause of a gerbil's bloody
nose is not the bedding, but the cage. Many a gerbil

has been known to rub his nose against the side of a wire cage out of curiosity or stress, resulting in a bloody nose. The remedy here is to apply antibiotic ointment to the nose for infection-fighting purposes and, perhaps, to switch to a less-abrasive housing situation. Consider, too, any changes you might make in the animal's daily routine to reduce stress and anxiety, such as moving the gerbil house to a quieter area of your home or keeping the family dog out of the gerbil's room.

Common Gerbil Illnesses

Despite their reputation for health and resilience, gerbils can and do fall victim to disease. Know what you're up against, and you'll be better able to safeguard your tiny pets' health.

TYZZER'S DISEASE

Probably the most feared and devastating disease to threaten pet gerbils is Tyzzer's disease, a highly contagious bacterial illness that can wipe out an entire household of gerbils.

The most notorious sign of this illness is diarrhea or even just a wet rear end, which is often accompanied by listlessness and a lack of appetite—though by the time these signs become evident, it may already be too late. An affected gerbil will typically die within twenty-four hours of the diarrhea stage, while in the meantime passing the disease on to his cagemates if they are not being protected with antibiotics. Indeed, as soon as you spot diarrhea in one gerbil, all the gerbils with whom that one has come into contact should start receiving antibiotics, for at this point of their exposure, they may still be saved. Thoroughly clean the gerbil house immediately, followed by wholesale cleanings every two days thereafter. That initial detection of diarrhea also, of course, warrants an immediate call to the veterinarian for assistance.

Tyzzer's disease is most common among gerbils subjected to filthy living conditions and stress—yet another reason why impeccable hygiene and a stress-free environment are critical to the keeping of gerbils. These elements, coupled with the attentions of an observant owner and quick veterinary action, can protect a gerbil, and an entire gerbil population, from suffering the perils of Tyzzer's disease.

EPILEPSY AND SEIZURES

The high incidence of seizures in gerbils is clear evidence that stress holds great power over these tiny animals. The good news is that, though seizures may be frightening to witness—the gerbil typically begins to twitch, he pins his ears back and may drool—in most cases, they are not serious.

Leave a seizing gerbil alone, try to keep the room quiet, and in a few minutes the condition will pass. The gerbil may be dazed for a moment, but before you know it, he'll be back to normal once more. Seizures are most common in young gerbils, particularly those under stress caused by rough handling and noise. Many grow out of them, especially when their owners change their ways and protect their pets from those stress-producing noises, overstimulation and rough or too much handling.

TUMORS

Once a gerbil reaches the age of 3, he is considered an elderly gerbil and may become prone to the development of tumors. Unfortunately, these are quite common in older gerbils and may crop up in the form of an unusual lump or bump anywhere on the body. Sometimes these are benign growths that are simply products of age, but the most common site for tumor development is on the scent gland on the underside of the gerbil's body. Located where you see a somewhat hairless region of the tummy area, this is the gland the gerbil uses to mark his territory and other gerbils, and tumors that develop there are fairly simple for the observant owner to detect.

While some veterinarians have been known to remove scent gland tumors surgically because they develop so close to the surface, this would seem a bit traumatic for a gerbil, who at an advanced age may not have much time left anyway. For most owners, who are comforted by the knowledge that tumors are relatively painless, the best remedy is to make sure affected gerbils remain content and comfortable until the end comes.

RESPIRATORY PROBLEMS

Gerbils are far more fortunate than their rat and mouse cousins where respiratory problems are concerned, as our gerbil friends are far less prone to breathing problems and infections of the respiratory system. When they do occur in gerbils, the cause is typically bedding-related, situations where gerbils are having bad reactions to the bedding material in their domicile. This is especially true if the bedding is of the cedar or pine variety, in which case it should be changed immediately to aspen, corncob, cellulose or paper bedding products.

Make sure to use proper gerbil bedding to prevent respiratory problems.

Respiratory infections are most likely to affect gerbils with compromised immune systems, particularly very young gerbils or older gerbils. Signs of infection or any respiratory condition typically include labored breathing (especially when accompanied by a clicking noise), listlessness, strange vocalizations and an unkempt coat. Though there are over-the-counter oral antibiotics that have proven effective in the treatment of some cases, antibiotics are best administered with the blessing and guidance of a veterinarian. In the meantime, you can help protect your gerbils from such problems by using the correct type of bedding and keeping humidity in the gerbils' atmosphere to a minimum by placing their domicile in a cool, dry place and watching out for spilled water dishes or leaky water bottles.

STROKE

Another condition common among older gerbils is stroke, and the classic sign of stroke is paralysis that affects one side of the animal's body. While multiple strokes can result in death, a gerbil that experiences a single event can often recover with little or no impairment as long as he can continue to eat and drink. Keep him warm and try to keep his stress (noise, rough handling and so forth) to a minimum. Even if he doesn't recover as completely as you wish he would, he can still live comfortably and contentedly, and when a gerbil is ill or injured, that's all we can ask for.

Enjoying
Your

part three

Gerbils

chapter 8

Understanding
Your
Gerbils

To this point, we have explored in depth just how delightfully gerbils can enhance our lives and make our homes such unexpectedly cheery places. We have also learned much about the caretaker's role in making this happen. Now we will explore just what makes the gerbil such a special little critter that we would want in our homes in the first place—in other words, why and how gerbils do what they do, and how we can use this increased understanding to better enjoy and care for these tiny animals.

The Language of Gerbils

Every animal species possesses its own unique language, and the gerbil is no exception. Once you have lived with a pair of gerbils for a while, you will no doubt be amazed at the complexity of their language as they communicate with one another throughout each day. And soon, if you behave yourself, you will realize that you, too, have been drawn into the fold. Not only will you find yourself becoming fluent in gerbil language, but also that you have become the recipient of those gerbil messages.

The most dramatic element in the gerbil's language is thumping, her practice of pounding her hind legs on the ground. If you happen to be in a room full of gerbils and one decides to thump, the experience can be rather startling when you realize, as sometimes happens, that all the other gerbils in the room have followed the originator's lead and are now all thumping in unison. But you also gain an even greater understanding of why this is occurring.

> ### TRANSLATING GERBIL THUMPING
>
> Part of gerbil language includes the thumping of her back feet. This can be a response to fear or amorousness, and this activity is completely normal. However, if you find your gerbils thumping a great deal, you may want to observe their environment to see if there is something consistently causing them fear. Keep in mind, too, that younger gerbils tend to thump more since they have less experience distinguishing what in their environment is safe and what is threatening.

Gerbils thump either when they are frightened or feeling amorous. In the former situation, you can see how the behavior could come in handy among a wild population: One gerbil detects a potential threat and sounds the alarm in the underground system of burrows she shares with her extended family. The thumping not only alerts the other gerbils by sound, but also by vibration. No one need miss the message. Indeed, this is the quickest and most efficient way that gerbils get each other's attention.

Because the reason for thumping is usually fear, you probably don't want your gerbils to be thumping all the time. But even a well-adjusted, well-cared-for gerbil can be frightened from time to time, and it's in your best interests and that of your pet to understand what is causing this behavior. You might also notice that younger gerbils tend to thump more often than older gerbils, and often for no apparent reason. This is because younger gerbils tend to be more skittish and more easily frightened than their elders. Just do your best to socialize your pets with frequent gentle handling, keep their environment as stress-free as possible, and in time the thumping should diminish.

Your gerbils' other behaviors won't be quite so dramatic, yet all are designed to strengthen the bond between the animals. A contented, well-acquainted pair of gerbils, for example, will spend their day snuggling, grooming themselves and each other, wrestling, chasing each other back and forth and napping in a ball all wrapped around each other.

Gerbils often express delight in seeing their owners by standing up against the wall of their enclosure.

Finally, if your gerbils have made you an honorary member of their family, when you walk into the room, you may notice that they stop what they are doing, run to the aquarium wall and stand up against the wall on their hind legs, begging you to reach in and pick them up so you can join in the bonding rituals. What an honor that is! Let the receiving of so high an honor be your goal.

Natural Behaviors

Gerbils also communicate through their natural behaviors, perhaps without quite even realizing that this is what they are doing. These behaviors are the evolutionary products of their lives as wild creatures in the arid lands of Mongolia. Seen in this light, we realize that, though these behaviors can be annoying, they are inherent tools of gerbil survival that do not vanish simply because the gerbils are living as pets in a contemporary home rather than struggling to survive in their wild homeland.

DIGGING

We want gerbils to dig. That's why we furnish their homes with a thick, clean layer of bedding. In fact, many believe it is actually cruel not to provide them with such an outlet to satisfy their natural digging impulses. But sometimes this digging behavior is elevated to such an extreme that you think your wee pet has been possessed by a digging demon that will not allow her to stop. This behavior typically takes place in the corner of her enclosure. She digs almost compulsively, leading a new gerbil keeper to believe that she is trying to escape. "What have I done wrong?" wails this unfortunate individual. Relax. It's not you. This is very natural behavior, known scientifically as "stereotyped digging," and it is nothing you need to worry about. It is the gerbil acting out ancient callings to expand the family compound. Just make sure the bedding is clean and of the proper material, and supply your pets with plenty of toys, which you may rotate from time to time, to help keep them distracted. Supply your gerbils, too, with a variety of hiding and nest boxes, including those of tubular shapes, such as PVC pipe segments and toilet paper rolls. And show your guilt the door.

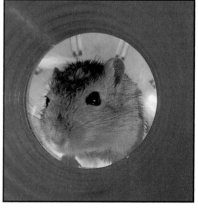

*Don't forget—
your gerbil loves
running
through tubes!*

TUMMY RUBBING

Let's say you walk into the gerbil room one day and you see one of your two female gerbils mounting the other female gerbil. You panic. The scene strikes the same fear in your heart that has stricken so many other gerbil owners before you, who suddenly realized that one of the gerbils they were told was a female is obviously a male. Relax. Odds are they are indeed both females, just as you were told. This is just an example of a gerbil's marking behavior. That bossy little female you witnessed mounting her cagemate was just proclaiming her dominance by marking her cagemate with secretions from her scent gland, a gland noticeable as a somewhat hairless patch on the underside of her body.

Enter another unique characteristic of the gerbil: the scent gland. It is standard equipment for both male and female gerbils, and they use it liberally to mark what they deem to be theirs, even if that happens to be another gerbil. The act obviously resembles what gerbils do to make little gerbils, but with this variety of mounting, you won't find yourself suddenly responsible for twelve gerbils instead of two—unless, of course, that little female you were told was a she really is a he after all. In that case, it's time to buy some more aquariums.

FIGHTING

Where fighting is concerned, gerbils are like dogs. Sometimes they fight for fun; it's part of their play routine, something they enjoy and something that keeps them both fit and reminded of their social order. But sometimes they fight for real—and sometimes to the death.

Play fighting is usually pretty obvious. The gerbils participate in a game that looks like "boxing," they tumble and wrestle a bit and will usually end up, once everyone is tired, falling into a mutual grooming session. Genuine fighting, on the other hand, is not nearly so pleasant. When two gerbils are on the verge of the real thing, you may notice one gerbil chasing the other aggressively, the chasee squealing a genuine sound of alarm and fear. Then, once they reach "the ball" stage, a serious battle has begun. When at war, gerbils will crunch themselves together into a ball and roll around in that tight circular position as they go viciously for each other's throat. You'll see fur, you might see blood, and you could end up with only one gerbil when it's over.

Even longtime established pairs have been known suddenly to declare war against each other, usually when one decides that it is now her turn to be the dominant gerbil. But true fights most commonly occur when an owner makes the foolish mistake of simply placing a new gerbil, an unfamiliar stranger, into a domicile belonging to an already established pair or otherwise established gerbil population. As we have seen, gerbils don't take to strangers, especially when those strangers are so abruptly introduced. You will see more later in this chapter about how to make proper introductions, but doing it this way will only result in chaos and injured gerbils.

Gerbil fighting behavior is further evidence why keeping an established same-gender pair is the superior arrangement for most pet owners. Anything else is just asking for a fight. If breeding is not your goal, then it's obvious why you would not want to house a male and a female together. The only other option for these very social critters is a same-gender situation, but usually not a group situation. While males have been known to cohabitate peacefully in groups from time to time, three's a crowd for females—and more than three is a catastrophe. Females, remember, are the dominant gender in the gerbil species, and they don't care to share their dominance, or their males, with each other. So protect your pets from their natural instincts, and remember that if fighting gerbils survive their altercation, it is usually impossible to get them back together again.

Fighting is a normal, usually harmless part of gerbil behavior, but watch for signs of real aggression like squealing and blood.

How to Tell the Boys from the Girls

You are just starting out as a gerbil caretaker, and you want to launch your journey right by getting yourself a

Enjoying
Your Gerbils

single-gender pair. You want to trust what you are told about the genders of the two animals you choose, but you also want to verify the situation yourself. Making such distinctions (a process called "sexing") in gerbils, as with most rodent pets, is not as easy as it is with dogs, for example, but there are signs you can look for that will help you rest easy.

Young gerbils are much more difficult to sex than those that are older than about 7 weeks of age. The optimum age for a young gerbil to leave her mother and enter her new home as a family pet is 6 to 8 weeks. Because this age can be a challenge to the sexing process, the identifications can get a little murky for

those looking for a same-gender pair, preferably siblings, who they hope will live happily, healthfully and without pups for years to come.

If you are working with an experienced breeder, you can probably rely on what he or she tells you. As for

Verifying your gerbils' genders is important if you want to avoid aggressive fighting and unexpected pups.

the teenage clerk at the local pet shop, well, that opinion could be a little more suspect. The expert knows to look for several signs. Females, for example, may have more prominent nipples on the undersides of their bodies, though this is no guarantee. Male gerbils also tend to be larger than females, but if the gerbils you are evaluating are not yet fully grown, this particular evaluation tool is somewhat ineffective.

A more technical sexing method involves taking a look at the gerbils' private areas—hardly your fondest dream, but necessary if you want to figure out what's what and who's who, and all part of your education as a gerbil owner. In fact, if you are purchasing your pets from an experienced, reliable breeder, he or she will probably give you a grand tour of the evidence as soon as you express interest in a given pair.

The easiest method for doing this is to hold the gerbil in your palm and gently lift up the rear end by the base of the tail (no holding the animal up in the air by the tail, please!). What you need to look for first is a bulge at the base of the gerbil's tail. While this bulge, the scrotum, will probably enlarge as the animal matures, thus making sexing much easier, it should be fairly noticeable on a young male, as well.

Now it's time to try what is considered the most reliable sexing technique—and one that the breeder will probably demonstrate to you with ease. While holding that little rear end up in the air, you will notice a hairless patch extending from the anus at the base of the gerbil's tail to the animal's genitals. The length of this patch of skin will be far shorter in a female than it is in a male. You may need to hold two gerbils side by side to see the difference (you'll need some extra hands to do this, of course). Even young gerbils can often be reliably sexed in this manner, but don't be ashamed about getting a second opinion. If you doubt your own evaluation abilities and those of the individual from whom you are buying the gerbils, feel free to stop by the office of your local (and experienced) veterinarian for a second opinion. When you're trying to start out right, it doesn't hurt to get all the information you can.

Introducing Newcomers

It's been made pretty clear by now that introducing strange new gerbils into an established population, even if that population consists of only one gerbil, is a big, potentially fatal, mistake. But this is not to say that it absolutely cannot be done. There is a method embraced by many experts in gerbil keeping that can be successful (although there are no guarantees), if the gerbil keeper is patient.

Before we get into more detail about this method, it's always wise first to evaluate the type of situation that is motivating you to embark on this risky venture. If, for example, you had an established pair—say, two males—and one died, and you really want to make sure that the surviving animal has the opportunity to

Enjoying
Your Gerbils

continue to be a social animal, then that is a legitimate reason. Another legitimate reason would be to reintroduce members of a once-established pair that have been apart for more than forty-eight hours.

On the other hand, if you have an established pair of female gerbils and thought it might be fun to add a third to create a trio (or, heaven forbid, you wanted to add a second female to a mated male-and-female pair), the mere thought of such foolishness is leading you and your gerbils down the road to disaster. If your motivation is that you have become attached to these adorable creatures and you would like to add more to the family, then do it the right way: Set up a whole new gerbil house and populate it with a new, compatible, same-gender pair.

On to our introduction method, commonly referred to as "the split-cage method," because it involves splitting a cage (or preferably an aquarium tank) down the middle to create two equal territories. Because the gerbil for whom you are seeking a companion will probably be an adult (young, sexually immature gerbils don't have as much trouble making new friends), the preferred candidate for that position would be a younger animal. Before you begin, both parties should be kept alone and isolated for a few days, so that loneliness and that natural longing for a buddy will set in.

The actual introduction process involves preparing a roomy aquarium with all the accoutrements and then dividing it in half, preferably with something made of a very fine mesh that will allow scents to pass through but will not facilitate aggressive behavior in the gerbils that could result in biting and toe injuries. You may even be able to find such a divider custom-made for your particular aquarium.

Place one gerbil in one side of the aquarium, and the other in the other side. Then you wait. And you rotate. Every few hours, gently pick up the gerbils and move each into the other's territory. Do you see what is going on here? You are forcing them, quite humanely, to get acquainted with each other's scents and with each other's presence without exposing them to direct contact with one another.

0Understanding
Your Gerbils

At first there may be some tension, especially if the gerbils are adult females. But after a few days, things should settle down as familiarity takes the place of suspicion and territoriality. Even when it seems all is peaceful, keep rotating your pets. This is where your patience plays a key role. Continue with this process for a minimum of one week, preferably for ten days to two weeks, just to be safe. Then, when your gerbils have convinced you that it's time, they may meet face to face on neutral ground (in other words, away from the split cage and in a safe, gerbil-friendly area).

If the gerbils immediately try to attack each other, then there is probably no hope for these two (remember, no guarantees). But if they seem friendly and inquisitive toward each other, perhaps even pleased to finally be meeting and greeting up close and personal, then you may be out of the woods, especially if this mutual admiration continues for the next half hour to an hour or so. Congratulations—you can probably count yourself, and your gerbils, victorious. The next step is to thoroughly clean the gerbils' new shared home, furnish it well, and move them in. Just to be on the safe side, you will still want to watch them for a few days to make sure you notice no signs of aggression or bites on their rear ends (signs of fighting that could escalate). What you're looking for is play behavior, mutual grooming, and lots of that signature gerbil snuggling at naptime. If you've made it this far, that's most likely what you'll see.

Gerbils and Predators

We've all seen those adorable photographs of a great big dog coming nose-to-nose with some tiny animal—a mouse, a hamster, a gerbil—held in the palm of someone's hand. Just look at the expression on the little critter's face. So curious. So fascinated. So paralyzed with fear.

Indeed, the gerbil's world is riddled with predators, including the creatures who care for them each day who are, in truth, the most deadly predators on the planet. There is much you can do, however, to neutralize the threat to your gerbil pets, both from yourself and from any other predators that might be living in your household.

Gerbils are not, of course, big, bold animals who greet the world with courage and aplomb. No, their survival depends on the "flight" side of nature's "fight or flight" response. When one's only fight mechanism is the ability to kick sand in someone else's face, well, we can see just why this timid little animal is more effective fleeing from danger than confronting it. But the gerbil is capable of sharing a wonderful bond with the people in his life. It all depends on whether those people are willing to work to make that happen.

Remember, no matter how safe you feel, in your gerbil's eyes, your cat, dog, snake or ferret is a predator.

First, handle your gerbils gently and carefully. Always. And approach them with fair warning. Remember that if you surprise them and sweep them up unexpectedly in your grasp, you are essentially no different from the huge birds that sweep down on gerbils in their desert homeland and carry them off to a grisly fate. That is no way to earn a gerbil's trust and respect. Commit this grievous error frequently enough, and you may never be able to regain your pets' esteem.

Once you have earned their trust by spending more and more time with them, speaking in a soft voice and handling them with an equally soft touch, you will no longer be the predator. Of course, your responsibilities as a convert also include protecting your pets from others of our species who may not be so enlightened: kids, kids' friends, your own friends who fancy themselves comedians at a small animal's expense. The gerbils must remain off-limits to anyone with less-than-worthy intentions—kids, adults and anyone in between. Convince your pets that, in your household, humans are not predators, and gerbils are treasured little beings.

Your home may also be occupied by other predators whose reputations will never be repaired as far as gerbils are concerned. These are, of course, the dogs and cats of the family—as well as any more exotic predators who may share your home, such as snakes and ferrets. Despite those charming photos where small animals sit petrified in paralyzed fear in the face of an animal that could and would willingly swallow them in one bite, gerbils were not put on this earth to be your dog's or your cat's best buddy. Sure, your dog may step forward and oh-so-sweetly lick the small animal that you hold in your hand, to which you respond with "Isn't that cute…he's kissing her." But the dog knows, and the gerbil knows, too, that what the dog is actually doing is *tasting* the gerbil, and that impulse will be a permanent one even if the dog is never allowed to act on it. So don't be naive.

This is not to say that dogs, cats, ferrets, snakes and gerbils cannot all share the same home. Just use some common sense and keep the gerbils in one section of the house (a quiet, somewhat secluded end) and the predatory animals in another. Even though cats, for example, may not have direct access to a resident gerbil because of an aquarium housing situation with a secured screen top, if cats are allowed access to the gerbil room at large, all that feline licking of the chops and pawing at the glass will petrify the gerbils with paralyzing fear, perhaps inspire seizures and strokes in the tiny animals, and subsequently open the door to all those serious stress-related gerbil health problems. Common sense is truly the better path to take—the path that allows all, regardless of species, to live happily ever after under a common roof.

chapter 9

Fun
with Your
Gerbils

Most people invite gerbils into their homes simply because they become enamored of these adorable creatures, their unique habits and expressions and the bit of nature they can bring into a contemporary urban or suburban household. But they also take that fateful step because they want to spend time with these little animals, enjoying their antics and delighting at the games gerbils play.

Of course you cannot embark upon this mission without a brief word of warning, the same word that has been preached throughout this book: trust. The gerbil is by nature a timid, easily frightened, easily stressed animal, who at first glance would not seem the ideal candidate for the role of rodent playmate. But that brings us to another unique and unexpected characteristic of this animal: He does want to play, and he does want to be as sociable with trusted owners as he is with his cagemate. The key word here, though, is "trusted." Success in forging a trusting relationship between human and gerbil hinges upon your behavior, how you treat and handle your gerbil. Those who do this with a quiet demeanor, a soft voice and a gentle hand will be amply rewarded with the opportunity to experience fun with gerbils. So, mind your p's and q's, and welcome to gerbil playtime.

Gerbil-proofing Your Home

We have already dealt with gerbil-proofing the gerbil's home, but what about the animal's time beyond the aquarium walls? The optimum gerbil lifestyle includes time spent now and then outside the gerbil's humble abode. Therefore, that region must be a safe environment for this tiny visitor—unencumbered freedom would be just asking for a lost gerbil or two. The key to that safety lies in the preparation. To begin preparations, choose a room in which you may play together.

Gerbils do not get along with phone cords and wires.

For obvious reasons (an overabundance of electrical cords, too many dangerous hiding places, extreme heat sources), the kitchen is probably not the safest choice. A bedroom, den or family room, on the other hand, probably would be an easier environment to gerbil-proof and to manage once your pet has entered to have some fun outside the confines of his humble gerbil abode.

Now, lie down on your stomach on the floor of the chosen room and look around to see what might pose a danger to a curious gerbil. There's always something—those live electrical cords behind that chair, for example, are just asking to be gnawed, possibly resulting in the electrocution of the unsuspecting gerbil gnawer. Even carpet that has come loose from a corner of the room can pose a danger should the gerbil decide that it, too, might provide a satisfying chewing experience.

Fabric of any kind, you remember, can choke a gerbil or cause intestinal blockage. And while you are evaluating the gerbil's safety, think about the safety of the items in the room, as well. For example, those valuable books you have stored on the lower level of the coffee table need to be moved to a higher elevation if you don't care to see them shredded by those phenomenal rodent incisors.

Now, take a look at the furniture in the room. Reclining chairs can pose a danger should a gerbil work his way into the interior and become a casualty when someone unknowingly slides the chair into its reclining position. Look, too, for holes in the back of the couch that will surely invite the attentions of a visiting gerbil seeking a cozy hiding place. You get the picture. Think like a gerbil, and evaluate what in the room might get a gerbil into trouble.

Access is another factor. When your gerbil is allowed to run freely, you must make sure that all doors to the room, including a sliding glass door to the back patio, are securely closed. This also means placing rolled towels at the bottom of each door to block even the smallest opening. Though your gerbil may trust and admire you completely, he will also be compelled by an ancient impulse inherent to all gerbils to explore and to escape. And, of course, all of a gerbil's time spent out and about in the world beyond the cage door must be

---

PREPARING YOUR GERBIL PLAY AREA

It's important for your gerbils to spend time outside their regular enclosure. Before you take your gerbils out to play, look out for the following:

- Electrical cords that might be gnawed on and cause electricution

- Fabric that may irritate the gerbils' respiratory system or intestines

- Any item at gerbil level that you absolutely don't want gnawed on

- Places in your furniture where your gerbils might hide and possibly be injured

- Doors and other "exits" where gerbils might escape

carefully supervised, both for his good and that of the many chewable, potentially expensive items he may encounter. Supervise always. No exceptions.

Safety also involves evaluating who will be in the room when a gerbil is frolicking there. When gerbil playtime rolls around, it's time for the family dog, cat, ferret and snake to be relegated to a different room—and time to make sure that they can't get back in during the gerbil's time out and about. No need to stress the poor tiny dear by subjecting him unnecessarily to the presence of predators when he is supposed to be having fun. You're trying to create fond memories, not tragic ones.

At Liberty

Now that you know that a gerbil can spend time outside his cozy home, what might you do with him during his time spent at liberty?

Even the slimmest of openings can be an escape route for gerbils.

Well, the answer depends on the gerbil and the relationship you share. You must first gain your pet's trust and convince him that he may depend on you to be both playmate and protector when he finds himself exposed and vulnerable. This bond is created through frequent gentle handling, quiet communication, and general interactions of every kind that convince the gerbil you are trustworthy.

You will typically know that you have reached this stage when you walk into the room, and your gerbils jump up against the side of their aquarium and beg for your attention. At that point, you can be fairly certain that you have succeeded in winning your pets' trust. Use that trust to enrich their lives even further by inviting them to partake of some fun new games and activities. The nature of these games and activities probably will continue to blossom as you spend more and more time with your pet, as you get to know what he likes and what he doesn't and as your own imagination works to expand your playtime repertoire.

While you will no doubt devise new games for you and your pet, there are some standard activities that are popular with most well-adjusted gerbils. Making his way through a simple maze, for example, can be both fun and stimulating for gerbils—and quite a novelty for onlookers to observe. Also popular among many gerbils is the so-called "hamster ball," a transparent plastic ball into which the gerbil can be comfortably placed, giving him the freedom to run and propel himself forward, backward, sideways...all around the room. This unique "vehicle" permits the gerbil to explore the world within the confines of a safe compartment, and it also gives him plenty of good cardio-vascular exercise.

Introducing new toys to your gerbil at play-time can give you both great pleasure.

Keep in mind, though, that not every gerbil will enjoy the hamster ball—or any toy, for that matter. And sometimes gerbils just don't feel like playing a usually favored game at a particular time. Like virtually every other animal on the planet, each individual gerbil has unique likes and dislikes. Some enjoy hamster balls, some don't; some enjoy making their way through mazes, some don't. Respect the differences, and don't force your pet to participate in an activity in which he is clearly not interested. That will only create stress for you both and cause tension in your relationship.

Another fun play idea is to provide your pet with a gerbil gymnasium within your chosen playroom. Place several toys within a high-sided container, such as a

20-gallon plastic storage box available at discount stores, or perhaps a child's wading pool. Some people even use a bathtub as a ready-made gerbil playground, or, as mentioned previously, a modular tube configuration enlisted for play rather than housing. Regardless of what you choose for the confines of your gerbil's gymnasium, throw a bit of clean bedding on the floor to prevent the animal from slipping and sliding. The toys you provide within this amusement park can include new and unique chew toys, a maze and perhaps an exercise wheel (remember, only a wheel designed for small animals with tails, one with solid sides and no spokes). This is not only a novel way of occupying a gerbil's time spent outside the cage, but it also increases the safety factors.

Playing outside his humble home can be a joyful time for the well-adjusted gerbil, but never underestimate the abundant pleasures of simplicity when you try to make playtime memorable. When all is said and done, the gerbil isn't most content with a dizzying variety of toys at his disposal, but with an owner he knows he can trust and with whom he enjoys spending his valuable time. While it can be a great pleasure to watch a gerbil hop about and play, your finest, most memorable moments may involve just sitting quietly with your pet as he perches happily on your shoulder and nibbles at your shirt. For many, such moments of quiet and mutual trust say it all.

How to Find an Escaped Gerbil

Even the most content and well-adjusted gerbil has been known to escape—sometimes from the best-planned, allegedly safe play and housing situations. While escapes seem most likely to occur when the gerbil is playing outside his cage, escapes from what you thought was a well-secured aquarium home are not uncommon (perhaps the screen top did not fit as tightly as you had thought?).

Your first challenge upon discovering a gerbil has escaped is to determine what room he is in. You may be 100 percent certain that he is in the room in which you were playing, or, to your horror, you may walk into the gerbil's room and discover an empty aquarium and have no idea where your little friend has gone. In this latter case, try walking through your home quietly, listening for soft gnawing sounds, and even letting out a sudden yell now and then to startle the small animal into making scampering noises that will help you pinpoint his whereabouts.

You must also prepare for your search. First, block all the exits in the house, preferably with a rolled towel at the foot of the door. Second, make sure all dogs, cats and other nonhuman predators are securely confined in a room that you are 100 percent certain is gerbil-free. Then, inform all the human members of the household of what has happened, and go on household alert. You must all use caution and care in your comings and goings—and even in your steppings. Finally, move all electrical cords and other such dangers off the floor to prevent an untimely tragedy.

There is no surefire method for luring a gerbil out of hiding. Again, it may all depend on the individual animal's habits and tastes. If, for example, your pet has a favorite treat (i.e., sunflower seeds), this is the time to pull out all the stops. But it is also the time to remain calm. You may sit quietly in the middle of the room in which you believe your pet is hiding and arm yourself with the favorite treat (surround yourself with them, in fact). You may also want to place a favored nest box on the floor should the escapee decide that he would like a cozy, familiar place to hide and rest for a while. You may even want to coo softly to the animal. Just your presence and that of the treats and other enticements may be all he needs to decide that being with you is far preferable to being a daring solo adventurer.

The same may hold true if his cagemate was left at home in the gerbil house. His longing for his companion—which may amplify by placing the gerbil house containing that equally lonely companion on the floor beside you—may also help to lure him out into the open, at which time you must resist the urge to shriek with delight. Instead, gently and quietly scoop him up and place him back safely where he belongs. Rest assured that once you have experienced the potential loss of a pet, there is little chance that you will ever allow it to happen again.

Why NOT to Breed for Fun

You may think it odd to discover a discussion of gerbil breeding in a chapter devoted to having fun with your gerbils. But given the fact that many people decide to take a stab at breeding their gerbils because they think "it might be fun," it should become clear to you why this section's inclusion makes sense.

What too many of these typically well-meaning people realize after it's too late—after they find themselves saddled with the care of ten new baby gerbils who will in weeks be old enough to start breeding themselves, and so on, and so on, and so on—is that maybe gerbil breeding isn't quite so fun after all.

Baby gerbils mean added responsibility for the owner.

Imagine, for example, how awful it would be to walk into the room where your happy little gerbil family resides and find one or both parents devouring the new babies. Fun, fun. Now, this is not the most common occurrence, but when gerbils are stressed, which could happen when they are being cared for by someone who isn't all that proficient or interested in caring for gerbil families, such a scene could be the unfortunate result. Sure, baby gerbils, or pups, can be adorable, and it's heartwarming to see both mom and dad looking after the kids—but what then?

We have explored the lightning-fast reproduction rates of gerbils and of the entire rodent family. Well, give that natural behavior a jump-start by housing a male and female together in domestic bliss, and before you know it, you could have an emergency population situation on your hands: too many gerbils, not enough space, not enough food, not enough money—and, worst of all, saddest of all, not enough homes to send the pups to when they come of age.

Gerbils are far from teetering on the brink of extinction, and they are not in any way difficult to find for the pet household. Why, then, do owners of pet gerbils feel the need to produce more gerbil pups and send them off into the world to fates and futures unknown? It's not as though mated pairs of gerbils are priceless fortunes in the making—what they are is inexpensive and plentiful. In our society, this translates not into "big fortune," but into "disposable pets." And we know how our species regards all things disposable. It's not pretty.

So why not just have fun with your gerbils in the purest sense: for who they are and not for how many little gerbils they might produce. Save yourself the panic that ensues when you absolutely cannot find homes for ten new little darlings—and for the ten more who will be following shortly thereafter. Resist the impulse to install a mated pair in your home, prevent the pitter-patter of little gerbil feet, and you take the most important step toward making sure that everyone—human and gerbil alike—will live happily ever after.

part four

Beyond the Basics

chapter 10

Resources

Organizations

The American Gerbil Society
www.geocities.com/Heartland/Shores/8181/AGS/

The Gerbil Club of Missouri
www.geocities.com/Athens/Acropolis/2582/GCM.html
16451 Forest Pine Drive
Wildwood, MO 63011

Gerbils International Association
http://members.aol.com/Ford6384/gia.html

The National Gerbil Society
(Please include self-addressed stamped envelope when writing)
Jackie Roswell (Secretary)
373 Lynmouth Avenue
Morden
Surrey, England SM4 4RY
www.rodent.demon.co.uk/gerbils/index.htm

Books

Holland, Laurie. *Gerbils...As a Hobby*. Neptune City, NJ: T.F.H. Publications, Inc., 1993.

Viner, Bradley. *All About Your Gerbil*. Hauppauge, NY: Barron's Educational Series, Inc., 1999.

Mail-order Catalogs

Many companies sell pet products through the mail. The companies listed below will send their catalogs free of charge.

Care-A-Lot Pet Supply Warehouse
1617 Diamond Springs Road
Virginia Beach, VA 23455
(800) 343-7680

Cherrybrook
Route 57, Box 15
Broadway, NJ 08808
(800) 524-0820

Discount Master Animal Care Catalog
Division of Humbolt Industries, Inc.
Lake Road, P.O. Box 3333
Mountaintop, PA 18707-0330
(800) 346-0749

General Animal Organizations

American Holistic Veterinary Society
2214 Old Emmerton Road
Bel Air, MD 21015

**American Society for the Prevention of Cruelty
to Animals**
424 East 92nd Street
New York, NY 10128-6804
www.aspca.org/

American Veterinary Medical Association
1931 North Meacham Road, Suite 100
Schaumburg, IL 60173-4360
www.avma.org/

The Humane Society of the United States
2100 L Street
Washington, DC 20037
www.hsus.org

International Veterinary Acupuncture Society
2140 Conestoga Road
Chester Springs, PA 18425

Massachusetts Society for the Prevention of Cruelty to Animals
350 South Huntington Avenue
Boston, MA 02130
www.mspca.org/

National Association of Professional Pet Sitters
1030 15th Street NW, Suite 870
Washington, DC 20005
(800) 296-PETS
www.petsitters.org/

Pet Sitters International Referral Hotline
(800) 268-SITS